MEHMET THE CONQUEROR
—— AND ——
CONSTANTINOPLE

A PORTRAIT OF YOUTH AND AMBITION

MEHMET THE CONQUEROR
── AND ──
CONSTANTINOPLE

A PORTRAIT OF YOUTH AND AMBITION

CHRISTOPHER EIMER

in loving memory of my mother Vera and parents-in-law Elin and Åke

First published in 2021 by Spink and Son Ltd

A CIP catalogue record for this book is available from the British Library.

ISBN 978-1-912667-66-6

Typeset by Russ Whittle

Printed and bound in Malta by Gutenberg Press Ltd

Spink and Son Ltd

69 Southampton Row

London WC1B 4ET

www.spinkbooks.com

CONTENTS

PREFACE

The fall of Constantinople, capital of Byzantium, on 29 May 1453, was to bring international recognition to twenty-one year-old Mehmet II (1432-1481) and the Ottoman Turks. Established a millennium earlier as the Eastern branch of the Roman Empire by Constantine the Great (r. 306-337 AD), the improbability of Mehmet's success, after failed attempts by various other factions, only added to the scale of the achievement.

Ascending the Ottoman throne as sultan in 1451, that early victory enabled Mehmet to establish an empire that would have a global footing by the time of his death, in 1481. Over the following five centuries, successive sultans would bring the dynasty yet greater political power, Constantinople having proved itself a strategic base of unparalleled advantage.

Sitting alongside Mehmet's success in battle was a propensity for portraits of himself by artists of merit. Dating from the 1470s and produced in a variety of genres, they have contributed to the enduring fascination in this challenging personality, while providing no sense of the victor at Constantinople twenty years earlier, for which very little material evidence of any kind was believed to exist.

It is against this backdrop that an unpublished circular bronze relief, bearing Mehmet's youthful, turbaned profile, was to come to light in 2000 (fig. 1).[1] Though unsigned, its stylistic treatment was entirely in keeping with fifteenth century medallic art of the Italian Renaissance, addressing its subject with Latin titles as the Great Prince and Great Emir, Sultan Master Mehmet: MAGNVS PRINCEPS ET MAGNVS AMIRAS SVLTANVS DNS MEHOMET. The absence of a design and lettering on the reverse was a less common feature of the genre, forestalling any immediate sense of the purpose bringing it into being; nor was there any stylistic indication of an artist's hand or workshop, to whom an attribution could readily be made.

At the time of its discovery, a well known posthumous medal of Mehmet II, made more than a century after his death, was undergoing study by Susan Spinale, a doctoral student at Harvard. As coincidence would have it, the portrait on the discovery piece represented the very prototype upon which that later issue had been based. It was made available to Spinale, who published it alongside her other findings in 2003. In 2012 the Ottoman scholar, Gülru

1. Unidentified artist: *Mehmet II, c.*1450, *Magnus Princeps* portrait, cast bronze relief, 91 mm.
(author; photo: Andrew Smart, A.C. Cooper Ltd, London).

Necipoğlu, was also to include it in a broad overview of Mehmet's portraiture. Various possibilities were explored by the respective authors, as to the circumstances bringing the bronze relief to fruition and its possible functions, both having speculatively placed its chronology in the 1460s.[2]

With the accession of Mehmet to the Ottoman throne and his conquest of Constantinople occurring a decade earlier, the question of where the chronology for the bronze relief could be accurately placed had a political imperative inviting further consideration. This was supported by the youthful appearance of its subject, the omission of any imperial titulature surrounding the portrait and the absence of any design or lettering on the reverse.

• • • • •

Philip Attwood, Peter Barber, Andrew Burnett, Robert Elderton, Cornell Fleischer, Neil Guthrie, Allan Hailstone, Stephen Scher, Geoffrey Schott and Raymond Waddington have generously offered insights, suggestions and clarifications covering many aspects of this work. Commissioned by Emma Howard at Spink, it has further benefitted from editorial and other assistance provided by Andrew Tortise, computer guidance of Nigel Colvert and a design by Russell Whittle. Esra Müyesseroğlu from the Topkapi Palace Museum in Istanbul kindly assisted in obtaining images. My dear wife, Missi, has been a constant help and support, without whom this book would not have come into being.

The bronze relief is generally referred to by its opening titles of *Magnus Princeps*, while the appellation of 'Mehomet', to be found on all the medallic portraits that he himself commissioned, has been used throughout the text in its abbreviated form of Mehmet. It leaves me to apologize for any errors, omissions and misinterpretations contained therein.

INTRODUCTION

Reflecting upon the manner in which the Ottoman conquest of Constantinople had brought an ambitious Muslim entity and its twenty-one year old sultan to international prominence, Cardinal Bessarion (1403-1472), the Latin patriarch of Constantinople, described the city of fabled splendour as having been 'despoiled, ravaged and sacked by the most inhuman barbarians, by the fiercest of wild beasts'.[3] He was far from alone in warning of the likelihood of further Ottoman attacks. It is by means of such reports that Mehmet the Conqueror would come to be known in the West.

Ascending the throne in 1451, Mehmet not only aggressively expanded Ottoman territorial reach over the following thirty years, creating an empire with an extensive trading network on both land and sea, but introduced an administrative structure that was similarly successful. It integrated the various elements of governance, such as land-tenure, commercial practice, penal law and the judiciary, constituting a blueprint for successive sultans in the continuing expansion of this dynastic power.

Mehmet II was born in 1432 in the then Ottoman capital of Edirne (Adrianople), situated some 150 miles west of Constantinople, the third son of Murad II (r. 1421-1451) and a mother who died in 1449 but whose origins, possibly Christian, are uncertain.[4] It was customary for Ottoman sultans to have their sons and heirs educated in the interior of Asia Minor, where they would act as local governors under the supervision of a reliable dignitary or advisor. Spending time in the Anatolian provinces at Amasya and Manisa in the early 1440s, Mehmet would gain administrative experience in governance.[5]

Both in those earlier years and subsequently as sultan, Mehmet sought to attract scholars in a broad range of academic disciplines, advising him on subjects as diverse as mathematics, astronomy, philosophy, geography and military engineering. His education also included the study of Christianity, Greek and Latin

opposite
2. Pisanello: *John VIII Palaeologus*, *c.*1440, cast bronze medal, 104 mm. (British Museum, Coins and Medals, London; Accession # G3, NapM.9).

and the reading of Arabic and Persian religious and literary classics.[6] Books and the development of libraries were considered an integral part of intellectual court life, while such knowledge was similarly necessary within an ever-expanding, interconnected world and the ambitious vision of an Ottoman empire.[7]

The contents of Mehmet's library, such as are known, reflect an interest in both East and West, with works variously acquired by booty or gift, as well as by commission. The range of material also includes more personal tastes, such as works on magic and a collection of sensationalist legends dealing with the foundation and antiquities of Constantinople.[8] An interest in manuscripts is confirmed by some ninety surviving examples dedicated to Mehmet himself, far exceeding those that can be associated with any other Muslim imperial patron. Of these, some twenty are on philosophy and a further five on logic, while related interests include decorative bookbinding.[9] Elements of this material were recorded in an extensive inventory by Mehmet's son Bayezid II (1447-1512).[10]

• • • • •

Mehmet's adolescence coincided with an evolution in relief portraiture in Renaissance Italy in the 1430s. Taking the form of a circular cast bronze flan of hand-held proportions, one side carried a portrait, usually taken in profile, around which would be placed the subject's titles. The reverse would similarly record details of relevance to the occasion of its making. As a means of preserving physical characteristics and biographical information in the permanence of bronze, the medal offered a celebration of the individual, as well as the sense of an after-life, previously available only to a nation's ruler and its coinage.

Interest in the classical past had been emerging over previous centuries in Italy and elsewhere in Europe through academic seats of learning and the work of esteemed writers. It was also to crystallize in the form of the Renaissance medal, whose iconographic roots lay in the coinage and medallic presentations of imperial Rome a millennium earlier.[11] This model of organizational prowess was one upon which the Ottomans were to fashion their own imperial enterprise.

Attracting patrons from many spheres of social and political life, initial designs for a proposed medal would be modelled in wax, from which a cast was made, usually in bronze, its surfaces having been tidied up and patinated. The various aspects of the medal making process required corresponding areas of skill, while humanists and scholars in related fields were on hand to advise on matters of style, form and convention. This added to the overall integrity of the work, but it was the inherent skill of an artist upon whom the veracity of the portrait ultimately depended.[12]

At the forefront of this artistic endeavour was the Italian medallist, painter and draughtsman, Antonio Pisano (c.1395-1455). Pisanello, as he is usually styled, cannot be said to have been the inventor of a genre with origins closely associated with the coinage and medallic issues of imperial Rome. He was, though, amongst the first to unify its various elements upon a larger diameter format, doing so with a masterful style and elegance, and in a manner that was to prove immensely popular.[13]

Within the humanist climate of Renaissance Italy, the portrait medal provided the opportunity for Pisanello's varied patrons to establish their own identity, as to how they saw themselves and wished to be seen by others. One of the earliest and most politically significant is a medal of John VIII (1392-1448), the penultimate Byzantine emperor and long-standing enemy of Mehmet's father, Murad II (fig. 2).[14] Commissions for Pisanello's medals, which were largely cast in bronze, but also in lead, came from a wide variety of patrons. Representing a prominent group, in their chivalric representation, were the dynastic rulers of Italian city-states. One of the first to be so portrayed was Filippo Maria Visconti, Duke of Milan (1392-1447), whose medal is thought to date to the second half of the 1430s (fig. 3).[15]

Other skilled exponents of low-relief sculpture were to emerge as pupils or followers of Pisanello. By the early 1450s, medal-making schools, studios and workshops had become established in Mantua, Florence, Naples, Ferrara and elsewhere on the Italian peninsula.[16] To one extent or another, these medals were exercises in propaganda, carrying not only a portrait, but a relevant design on the reverse, to be cast and distributed in varying numbers. The celebrity of the patrons themselves, as well as any underlying political elements, would determine whether re-castings of a particular medal might be made over subsequent years as well as further copies of those casts. In less common instances, a medal intended for personal or private purpose might well constitute circumstances that did not require more than one casting, nor even a design or lettering on the reverse.

• • • • •

Believed to be amongst the earliest of the portraits of Mehmet is a medal by the

painter and medallist, Costanzo di Moysis da Ferrara (1450 - after 1520). The artist had been summoned from Naples to the Ottoman court in Istanbul to take the sultan's portrait, though the chronology for this visit is uncertain, as indeed are the artist's precise origins (fig. 4).[17] Known from a single bronze cast in the National Gallery of Art, Washington D.C., the Latin titles refer to Sultan Mehmet, Emperor of the Ottoman Turks, as the thunderbolt of war having laid low peoples and cities: SVITANVS MOHAMETH OTHOMANVS TVRCORVM IMPERATOR (obverse) / HIC BELLI FVLMEN POPVLOS PROSTRAVIT ET VRBES. CONSTANTIVS F (reverse). The portrait itself conveys a sense of self-aggrandisement perfectly in keeping with its overall message of triumph. Although knowledge of Costanzo's movements is insufficient to confirm the precise chronology of this medal, Mehmet's appearance suggests someone in their forties, which would place the work in the mid-1470s.

The Venetian artist Gentile Bellini (1429-1507) is among the most celebrated artists to have visited the Ottoman court, following what may have been a diplomatic approach, arriving there in 1479. Bellini had been the official painter to the Venetian Republic and produced what has become the most well known representation of Mehmet II. In oil on canvas and dated on its frame 25 November 1480, it was acquired more than a century ago by the National Gallery in London (fig. 5).[18]

The signature of Gentile Bellini also occurs on a medal of Mehmet that is known from several bronze casts (fig. 6). The Latin titles MAGNI SVLTANI F MOHAMETI IMPERATORIS (obverse) / GENTILIS BELLINVS VENETVS EQVES AVRATVS COMES Q PALATINVS F (reverse) address him as the Great Sultan Emperor Mohamet, while the reverse illustrates three vertical crowns – echoing those on his portrait of Mehmet in oil – and refers, in the making of the medal, to the Venetian, Gentile Bellini, Golden Knight and Palace Companion.[19] It is possible that some specimens of Bellini's medal were cast during his sojourn at the Ottoman court, prior to Mehmet's death in 1481. Others may have been produced

opposite
3. Pisanello: *Filippo Maria Visconti, Duke of Milan*, *c*.1435-1440, cast bronze medal, 103 mm. (National Gallery of Art, Washington, D.C.; Samuel H. Kress Collection, # 1957.14.595).

(obverse)

4. Costanzo da Ferrara: *Mehmet II*, c.1475, cast bronze medal, 123 mm.
(National Gallery of Art, Washington, D.C.; Samuel H. Kress Collection, # 1957.14.695).

(reverse)

4. Costanzo da Ferrara: *Mehmet II, c.*1475, cast bronze medal, 123 mm.
(National Gallery of Art, Washington, D.C.; Samuel H. Kress Collection, # 1957.14.695).

5. Gentile Bellini: *Mehmet II, c.*1480, oil on canvas, 48 x 65 cm. (National Gallery, London; # NG 3099).

6. Gentile Bellini: *Mehmet II*, *c*.1480, cast bronze medal, 94 mm.
(National Gallery of Art, Washington, D.C.; Samuel H. Kress Collection, #1957.14.737).

by the artist on his return to Venice, as a commercial project for those wanting a portrait taken by someone with first-hand knowledge of the sultan.

The Florentine artist Bertoldo di Giovanni (c.1440-1491) produced a medal of Mehmet II in bronze, which is similarly known from a number of casts and thought to date to around 1480 (fig. 7). The Latin titles MAVMhET ASIE AC TRAPESVNZIS MAGNE QVE GRETIE IMPERAT (obverse) / GRETIE / TRAPESVNTI / ASIE / OPVS BERTOLDI FLORENTIN SCVLTORIS (reverse) refer to the sultan as Emperor of Asia and Trebizond and Magna Graecia. The reverse features a complex political allegory that alludes to those territories and carries the signature of Bertoldo.[20] The artist was closely attached to the court of Lorenzo de' Medici (1449-1492), but it is not clear whether the medal was commissioned by Lorenzo for Mehmet as a form of diplomatic gift as well as an

7. Bertoldo di Giovanni: *Mehmet II*, c.1480, cast bronze medal, 94 mm.
(National Gallery of Art, Washington, D.C.; Samuel H. Kress Collection, # 1957.14.842).

8. Unidentified artist: *Mehmet II*, *c*.1475-80, watercolour and gold paper, 21 x 26 cm.
(The Presidency of the Republic of Turkey, Directorate of National Palaces Administration;
Topkapi Saray Museum, Istanbul, # TSMK, H. 2153, fol.145).

expression of Florentine medallic work, or whether it represents an independent request from the sultan for a medal by such an artist. On first sight, the portrait is stylistically similar to that on the medal by Bellini (fig. 6), but there are sufficient differences in the subtleties of modelling to warrant the consideration of an entirely different source, perhaps originating from a drawing carried to the Florentine court by an emissary from Constantinople.

A watercolour on paper in the Topkapi Palace Museum, Istanbul, which is thought to date from the mid- to late 1470s, carries a full profile of the sultan set against a gold background (fig. 8).[21] It has clear Western stylistic links in its treatment of the portrait and drapery, as may be seen in Costanzo's medal (fig. 4). Another watercolour portrait on paper, also in the Topkapi Palace Museum, depicts Mehmet II smelling a rose (fig. 9). The three-quarter facing portrait conveys an awkward manner of figuration and more readily suggests an artist unschooled in the Western tradition of perspective. The mixture of stylistic endeavours has created difficulty in establishing a chronology, though one that scholars have tended to position towards the end of the sultan's reign.[22]

Following Mehmet's death in 1481, Costanzo was to produce a revised version of his medal (fig. 10).[23] This deploys a somewhat similar portrait and titles to those used on his earlier medal (fig. 4): SVLTANI MOHAMMETH OCTHOMANI VGVLI BIZANTII INPERATORIS 1481 (obverse) / MOHAMETH ASIE ET GRETIE INPERATORIS YMAGO EQVESTRIS INEXERCITVS. OPVS CONSTANTII (reverse). It refers to Mehmet as Emperor of Asia and Greece, riding on campaign. Known from a small number of contemporary casts and some later castings, this medal may be seen as an initiative on behalf of Bayezid II to honour his father's memory as emperor of Byzantium. As news of Mehmet's death began to permeate to the outer world, no doubt greeted with joy as well as sorrow, castings of the medal may have also catered to commercial interests for such a portrait.[24]

9. Unidentified artist: *Mehmet II Smelling a Rose*, *c*.1475-80, watercolour on paper, 27 x 39 cm.
(The Presidency of the Republic of Turkey, Directorate of National Palaces Administration;
Topkapi Saray Museum, Istanbul, # TSMK, H. 2153, fol. 10).

(obverse)

10. Costanzo da Ferrara: *Mehmet II*, 1481, cast bronze medal, 120 mm.
(Victoria & Albert Museum, London, Salting Bequest, A.208-210).

(reverse)

10. Costanzo da Ferrara: *Mehmet II*, 1481, cast bronze medal, 120 mm.
(Victoria & Albert Museum, London, Salting Bequest, A.208-210).

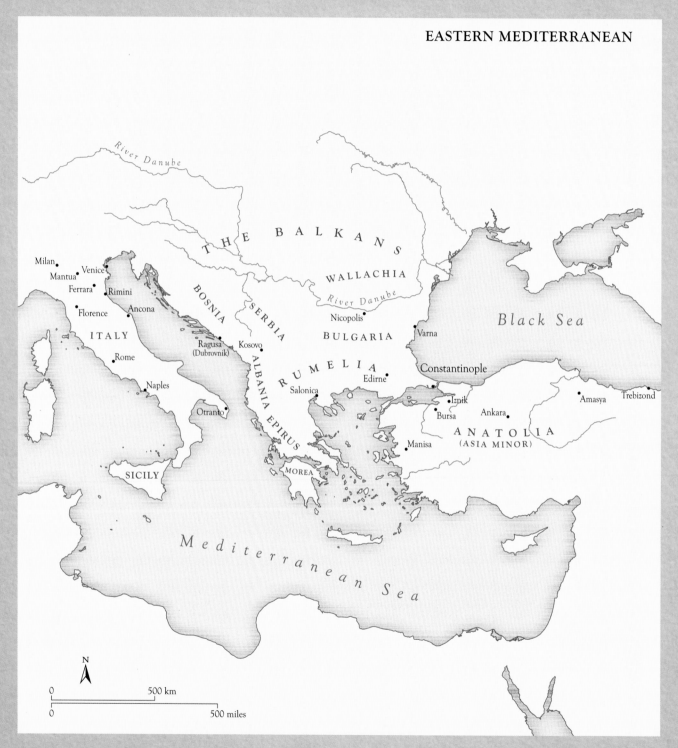

EASTERN MEDITERRANEAN

River Danube

THE BALKANS

WALLACHIA

River Danube

BOSNIA

SERBIA

BULGARIA

Nicopolis

Varna

Black Sea

Milan

Mantua   Venice

Ferrara   Rimini

Florence   Ancona

ITALY

Ragusa
(Dubrovnik)   Kosovo

Rome

RUMELIA

ALBANIA EPIRUS

Constantinople

Edirne

Naples

Salonica

Otranto

Iznik

Amasya   Trebizond

Bursa   Ankara

ANATOLIA
(ASIA MINOR)

Manisa

SICILY

MOREA

Mediterranean Sea

N

0 _____ 500 km

0 _____ 500 miles

Prepared by Helen Stirling

I

SECURITY AND SUCCESSION

There appears to be no defining genealogical source for the Ottomans, who were one of several Muslim nomadic tribes to emerge in the late 1200s or the early 1300s. Occupying territory in north-west Anatolia, on the frontiers of the Islamic world, they found themselves within a migratory junction between Asia Minor and Europe. One of its earliest representatives is thought to have been a Turcoman tribal chieftain called Osman, who is believed to have died around 1324.[25] He attracted a growing number of warriors and others wishing to join his expanding polity, which was to demonstrate an increasing hunger for territorial gain.[26]

In their successful expansion over following decades, the Ottomans were to occupy provinces formerly governed by Byzantium in Asia Minor and the Balkans. Amongst some of their more prominent early campaigns were the conquests of Bursa in 1326, which would form one of the capitals, Nicaea (Iznik) in 1331, and Kosovo in 1389, which represented an important victory over the Serbs. It was the first major success of Bayezid I (r.1389-1402), great-grandson of Osman and great-grandfather to Mehmet the Conqueror. Bayezid was to achieve a yet more significant victory at Nicopolis in 1396 against the Hungarians, giving the Ottomans control of the Balkans and broadening their political influence yet further.[27] Bayezid was to spend most of his reign on campaigns, enlarging Ottoman domain towards the east and the west, including much of the territory that had once belonged to the Eastern Roman Empire of Byzantium.

Bayezid had attempted to lay siege to Constantinople between 1394-1402, with what was to be the first of two unsuccessful Ottoman attempts on the Byzantine capital. Despite that failure, his success at Nicopolis and other territorial gains were to significantly raise the family's prestige in the Islamic world and help create the beginnings of a centralized empire. A century later it would stretch from the Danube to central Anatolia.[28] At a decisive battle in 1402 outside Ankara, between the Ottomans and the nomadic conqueror Timur (r. 1370-1405) – who had spent the previous two decades building a vast empire on the Mogul model – Bayezid was taken prisoner and died soon after. Although Constantinople would remain an unrealized ambition, he had placed the Ottomans on a firm foundation and would come to be acknowledged in various ways by his great-grandson Mehmet.

Bayezid's death had left the question of Ottoman succession unresolved and a complex struggle for power soon emerged, played out by just a few of his many sons, including Suleyman (r.1402-1411), Musa (r.1411-1413) and Mehmet I (r.1413-1421). With other sons scattered in different parts of the sprawling empire, there ensued an eleven-year period of family war, considered amongst the most destructive in Ottoman dynastic history, following which Mehmet I succeeded as sultan in 1413.[29] A century earlier, Osman had deliberately given the reins of power to his son Orhan (r.1324-1362), thus leaving no realistic opportunity for others to contest the choice of heir to the throne.[30] Similarly desirous of ensuring an untroubled transfer of power, Mehmet I appointed his son Murad II as heir to the dynasty.

Despite such difficulties, continuing territorial expansion had enabled the Ottomans to occupy two cities as capitals: at Bursa, lying to the east in Anatolia, and at Edirne, to the West in Rumelia. Murad II was to begin his reign in 1422 with another failed attempt on Constantinople, but in 1430 he launched a series of successful campaigns conquering Salonica, Morea, Epirus, Albania and Serbia. This would considerably enlarge Ottoman domination in Europe.[31]

Muslim challenges to the Byzantine Empire and its capital of Constantinople had endured over centuries, but it had taken no more than a few decades for the Ottomans to emerge in the 1430s as the main instrument of that challenge. Their increasing territorial supremacy under Murad II corresponded with the gradual disintegration of an empire owing its legacy to imperial Rome. It was an empire that dominated the Eastern Mediterranean for more than a millennium, protecting trade routes and forming a line of defence for the Christian West against Islam.

An international forum, convened at Ferrara in 1438, sought a reconciliation of the Eastern and Western churches and a universal crusade against growing Ottoman imperialism. The Council of Ferrara – which would move to Florence in 1439 owing to plague – was convened by the Venetian pope, Eugenius IV (r.1431-1447), and amongst its principal delegates was the Byzantine emperor, John VIII, accompanied by a vast entourage.[32] With Constantinople increasingly unable to rely upon its Western allies for protection, and the West in general vulnerable to Ottoman attack, the proceedings at Ferrara reflected an existential crisis of significance to many. It had attracted an international gathering with varied political and cultural interests, among whom were antiquaries and artists, including the medallist Pisanello. He was to produce a series of drawings, recording some of the delegates, including John VIII resplendent in the exotic robes of his office.[33]

Pisanello's medal of John VIII is believed to have been produced a year or so after the opening of the Council of Ferrara. It shows him wearing a distinctive tall, conical hat with an upturned, pointed brim, while the reverse represents the emperor's equestrian figure (fig. 2). As head of the Byzantine Empire, the encircled titles in Greek affirm John VIII's status as 'King and Emperor of the Romans', this being the traditional reference for the holder of that office.[34] There is some uncertainty as to the exact source for this commission, which may have been Pope Eugenius IV. The medal was cast in bronze and lead, in an unknown number of specimens, and is amongst Pisanello's most remarkable, with regards to the circumstances of

conception, the graphically expressed iconography, and its veiled political remit.

The despatch by John VIII of embassy officials and envoys to Venice and Rome, in early 1442, represents one of the means by which casts of Pisanello's medal may have been distributed within Italy and beyond its shores.[35] The inclusion of Pisanello's signature in both Latin and Greek might be seen as a gesture towards John VIII, being both the Roman and the Byzantine emperor. With the political concerns arising from increasing Ottoman power, Pisanello's medal constituted an ardent and sincere 'expression of hope' for Christian victory in the East.[36]

• • • • •

The Councils of Ferrara and Florence would achieve little, with Ottoman incursions continuing to imperil Byzantine territory. Though failing in his own attempt on Constantinople twenty years earlier, Murad II was to gain a particularly significant victory in November 1444 against the united forces of the Hungarian-Polish and Walachian armies at Varna in Eastern Bulgaria. It was to raise the Ottoman profile in the West yet further and diminish the threat of retaliation by Christian crusade.

The decade-long family war of succession, which followed Bayezid I's death in 1402, was to remain a fresh memory forty years later. Adding to that sense of insecurity were notoriously loose tribal loyalties and the threat of hostage taking. With sons from various wives scattered far and wide, it raised the possibility of claimants to the Ottoman throne appearing at any time. The Byzantines had themselves attempted to take advantage of the Ottoman succession struggle by harbouring its princes as diplomatic hostages.[37]

These were some of the circumstances that had encouraged Murad II to secure the line of succession and establish Mehmet as his successor at the earliest opportunity. By Spring 1444 the twelve year-old would serve as regent of the province of Rumelia, under the supervision of the family's trusted grand vizier, Chandarli Halil Pasha (d.1453), scion of an illustrious Turkish family of the old Ottoman ruling class, whose members had served and advised successive sultans.[38]

• • • • •

During a period when crusader invasions and other crises threatened to destroy the Ottoman empire altogether, and within shifting political frontier regions, Constantinople remained the only secure option for the Ottomans to propagate their long term imperial aspirations. It more broadly represented an inveterate dream and cherished goal for numerous medieval Muslim polities, having been established as the Eastern outpost of the Roman Empire by Constantine the Great in around 320 A.D. (fig. 11).

This bulwark between Christianity and Islam was as rich in historical precedent as it was alive with prophecy, over which an aura of superstition hung like a permanent mist. It had featured in sacred and secular Muslim legend over centuries, having fuelled apocalyptic fears and expectation across the entire Islamic world.[39] The Ottoman dynastic house was aware of the eschatological and prophetic significance of the Byzantine capital, its conquest having been considered one of the feats to be accomplished by the messianic conqueror as the ultimate phase of history.[40] A *hadith*, featuring amongst the sayings attributed to the Prophet Muhammad, ordained that 'Verily they will conquer Constantinople. Truly their commander will be an excellent one. Truly that army will be an excellent one!'.[41]

Over many centuries, Muslim scholars and men of science sought the opportunity of determining events through the alignment of the stars and other celestial phenomena. With the use of astrolabes and other forms of instrumentation, horoscopes and written charts would contribute to the Ottoman historical imagination and political culture. With its focus upon lineage and empire building, astrology could indicate the most propitious time for an Ottoman royal birth, just as it could an imperial enterprise or military campaign.[42] Murad II's victory against the crusader forces at Varna in 1444 was seen as one such apocalyptic occurrence, but the final one was to be the conquest of Constantinople itself.[43]

The loss to Byzantium in 1448 of its emperor John VIII, shortly followed in 1451 by the Ottoman loss of Mehmet's father, Murad II, contributed to this sense of apocalyptic urgency.[44] For Muslims, Christians and Jews alike, the conquest of Constantinople represented the realization of a prophecy with universal appeal. As the inheritors of both Byzantine and Islamic apocalypticism, the Ottomans were no less influenced by this imperative. It represented a rich and popular intellectual

tradition, extending throughout the Byzantine Empire, whereby the end of empire was associated with the end of the world.[45] More immediately, however, Constantinople offered the Ottomans a strategic gateway between the Eastern Mediterranean and the Black Sea.

It is against this broader scenario that Mehmet's elevation to power took place in 1444, following which he would begin to exercise increasing authority. The belief that Constantinople held a pretender to the Ottoman throne may have been responsible for fuelling an ill-conceived attempt on the Byzantine capital by the young and ambitious sultan. The details themselves are unclear, but from 1446

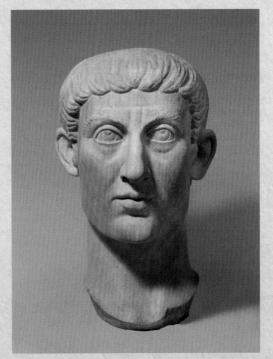

11. Unidentified artist: *Constantine the Great*, marble bust, AD 325-370
58.4. cm. height, 67.3 cm. depth.
(Metropolitan Museum of Art, New York; Mary Clark Thompson, # 1923. 26.229).

Mehmet would serve in a provincial capacity as a governing crown prince in Manisa, Western Anatolia, where Murad II had built a palace.[46]

• • • • •

The imperial authority provided by titulature in its various forms was important to any fledgling political enterprise. Little such epigraphic evidence survives from the early Ottoman period, although an endowment deed of 1324, composed in Persian, mentions sultan Orhan and his recently-deceased father, Osman, providing for them the respective epithets of 'Champion of the Faith' and 'Glory of the Faith'. Titles were of relevance in establishing an identity, with Orhan having found it no less opportune to make the 'significant political statement of sovereignty' that was implied in the striking of coinage.[47] A century later, in the mid-1440s, coinage struck in the joint names of Murad and Mehmet was to confirm their dual sovereignty. Produced at various mints, including those at Amasya, Bursa and Edirne, and observing aniconographic tradition, these coins, ten millimetres or so in diameter, carry text

12.1 (Amasya).

12.2 (Bursa).

12.3 (Edirne).

12.1-12.3: Ottoman silver coinage from the years 1444-1445 AD (848-849 H); diameters between 9 mm. and 11 mm. (F.R. Künker of Osnabrück, Auction 231, 16 March 2013, Lots 9080, 9081 and 9083).

alone, with no portraits or figural designs. Small though they may have been, they had nonetheless left the question of Murad's choice of heir to the Ottoman succession in no doubt (figs. 12.1-12.3).[48]

Official documents were another means of propagating titular authority. An Ottoman treaty with Venice in February 1446, upon which Mehmet is co-signatory with his father, refers to him in its Latin nomenclature as MAGNVS PRINCEPS ET MAGNVS AMIRAS SVLTANVS MEHOMET BEY [Great Prince and Great Emir, Sultan Mehmet Governor]. Notably similar in formula to that encircling Mehmet's portrait on the *Magnus Princeps* bronze relief, the use of such titles more broadly points to his desire of expressing status and position whenever such opportunity presented itself. On the death of his mother in 1449, Mehmet is reported to have commissioned a burial casket carrying the self-styled titles of 'Homonym of the Prophet and Noble Lord'.[49]

Although Mehmet would have to wait until the death of his father, Murad II, in 1451 before he could assume absolute authority, he was already considering himself a sultan in his own right during that five-year interregnum. In the winter of late 1450, after a decade of almost constant warring, Murad II finally retired, his death just a few months later, in February 1451, having paved the way for nineteen year-old Mehmet's formal accession at Edirne. A retrospective view

13. Nakkas Osman (by or after): *Accession ceremony of Mehmet II* in 1451 (retrospective view, *c*.1580), watercolour on paper, 33.5 cm. x 49.5 cm. (The Presidency of the Republic of Turkey, Directorate of National Palaces Administration; Topkapi Palace Museum, Istanbul; # TSMK, H.1523, fol. 153b (v) Hünername, vol. I).

of the ceremony in watercolour is believed to have been produced in the 1580s (fig. 13).

Pisanello had demonstrated the adaptability of a medium that was being received with growing enthusiasm by Western patrons, who were now able to manipulate a sense of 'classical triumph' in bronze relief.[50] Sigismondo Malatesta (c.1417-1468), the Riminese overlord, was to prove a particular adherent of the genre, seen here on a medal by the master, produced c.1445 (fig. 14).[51]

Among the more celebrated medal makers to follow in Pisanello's footsteps was Matteo de' Pasti (fl.1440-1467), who was also to produce a medal of Sigismondo Malatesta in the late 1440s or early 1450s (fig. 15).[52] Cast in large numbers and carrying a portrait of Sigismondo on one side and a representation of his castle at Rimini on the other, this is de' Pasti's most prolific medal. It graphically represents the means by which Sigismondo chose to communicate his status to subjects, allies and enemies.[53] Bearing the date of 1446, which is when he dedicated his new castle, it also demonstrates the means by which the medal could affirm position,

14. Pisanello: *Sigismondo Malatesta*, c.1445, cast bronze medal, 89 mm. (National Gallery of Art, Washington, D.C.; Samuel H. Kress Collection, # 1957.14.604).

power and identity. Made in at least two varieties, with one showing Sigismondo wearing armour rather than drapery, specimens were not only distributed, but used as a form of talisman, buried within the fabric of his castle.[54] Other such forms of communication that Sigismondo deployed, in order to advance his political and cultural status, include the distribution of classically inspired literary works, of which Mehmet is noted as having been a recipient.[55]

Fifty years after Bayezid I formulated his plans for an empire with Constantinople at its centre, Mehmet had been presented with an opportunity of embodying his universal ambition, as heir to the kingdom of New Rome, in a manner which neither Ottoman coinage nor written documents could satisfy.

15. Matteo de' Pasti: *Sigismondo Malatesta*, *c*.1450, cast bronze medal, 80 mm. (National Gallery of Art, Washington, D.C.; Samuel H. Kress Collection, # 1957.14.654).

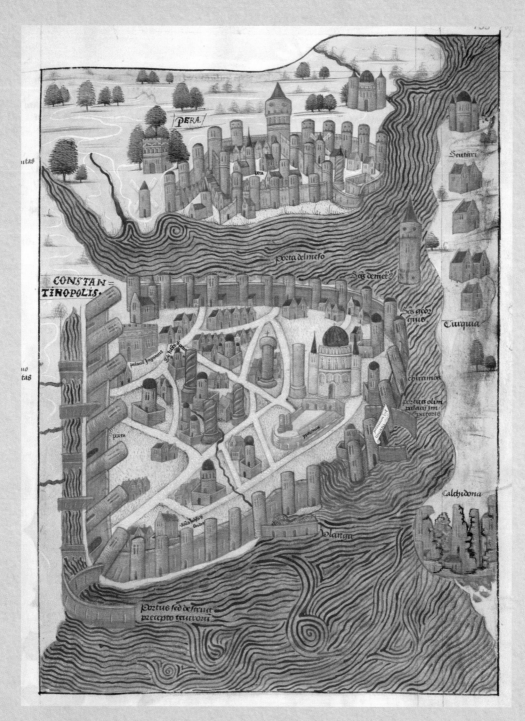

Map of Constantinople and Pera taken from *Liberum Insularum*, c.1485, based on Cristoforo Buondelmonte's plan, prepared on his visit in c.1420. (British Library Board, Arundel Ms. 93.f.155)

2

ARTIST AND SITTER

Mehmet had been attracted to a genre that could be considered a natural 'heir to the forms and implications' of ancient coinage.[56] With bronze the favoured metal and Latin the favoured language, an immediate connection was provided between the medallions and sestertii of the Roman Empire and the Renaissance medal.[57] A medallion of the emperor Commodus (161-192 A.D.) offered one such model, amongst a vast array of stylistic choice (fig. 16).

The *Magnus Princeps* bronze relief of Mehmet fully concurs with the physical characteristics of the Renaissance medal, including variations that naturally arise from the process of heat and metal casting (fig. 1). Taken at different points of the circumference, its diameter ranges between 90 mm. and 92 mm., while a scientific analysis of the fabric itself reveals large constituents of copper as well as small elements of tin and lead, in keeping with the consistencies expected of the genre.[58] Coming to notice in 2007, seven years after the bronze relief had appeared, was a specimen in lead (fig. 17).[59] Debased metal

did not lend itself for coinage and was otherwise thought a material not worthy for courtly exchange, though it could usefully serve as an artist's proof or model.[60]

Light speckling across both sides of the bronze relief indicates its process of

16. Unidentified artist: *Commodus*, A.D. 186-190, bronze Roman medallion, 40 mm. (British Museum, Coins and Medals, London; # 1850, 0276.1).

facture to have been that of sand-casting, while small dark deposits – visible for example in the field before Mehmet's face – represent residual evidence of the original wax model upon which the portrait had been created. The remnant of a guidance line beneath the word *Mehomet*, employed on the model to help position the lettering, is another legacy of the artist's hand and also present, in a corresponding position, on the lead proof. The surfaces of the bronze relief have a deep, reddish-brown patina, and while there is a degree of light, natural wear across Mehmet's portrait, it is largely as it left the artist's workshop, entirely free of tooling or chasing.

• • • • •

A tightly wound turban covers the upper part of Mehmet's head, its narrowness and forward rake exposing a closely cropped area to the rear.[61] Amidst the crown of the turban is a woven cap of lace form. The outer elements of the cap are decorated with a calligraphic pattern, from which a small feather projects. Emerging from beneath the turban are tightly-formed side-locks that continue to a full but narrowly formed beard and moustache.

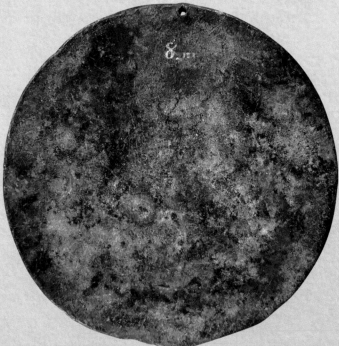

17. Unidentified artist: *Mehmet II, c.*1450, *Magnus Princeps* portrait, cast lead relief, 91 mm. (author).

The sultan wears a distinctively patterned and heavily-textured kaftan, with four fastenings and a fur-trimmed collar. Beneath the kaftan is another garment of indiscernible form.[62] These elements have all been sensitively modelled, with regard to the lively characterization of the portrait and the intricacy of the multi-layered garments.

The perpendicular alignment of Mehmet's portrait has been facilitated by a small and carefully positioned piercing. This is a ubiquitous feature of the Renaissance medal, which often masks elements of the design, while less commonly enabling the portrait to be seen in its natural position. Due consideration must have been given to the placing of the piercing, which, coincidentally or not, divides the forty-six lettered inscription in equal measure.[63] These parameters are identical on the lead relief.

Seen side by side, the bronze and lead reliefs reveal no differences in the modelling of the portrait, although Mehmet's profile appears to be more gaunt on the lead, while his beard appears to be thicker on the bronze. This can be explained by natural inconsistencies of metal flow during the casting process, whereupon the 'h' and 'o' of *Mehomet* appear to be conjoined on the bronze, but separated on the lead. Their respective diameters, taken from fixed internal points, are identical in every respect.[64]

• • • • •

There are no immediate indications as to precisely when the commission of the *Magnus Princeps* bronze relief took place, but the benefit of other portraits of Mehmet, as well as eye-witness accounts and the broader political landscape, provide a relatively narrow window in which to consider the chronology.

An unattributed contemporary account makes a reference to Mehmet's 'just-grown youthful beard' and 'proudly raised' head.[65] These allusions to youth and an unfamiliar posture accord with the *Magnus Princeps* profile. Aligning with those characteristics is a recent reference to the portrait as the 'most reliable indicator' of the sultan's appearance in his youth, which concurs with someone in their late teenaged years or early twenties.[66] A clear sense of change in Mehmet's appearance over the following decade is apparent from an account in 1458 by Giacomo de' Languschi (fl.1435-1460), a Venetian emissary at the Ottoman court. It refers to Mehmet, now twenty-six years old, as having 'well-built' proportions and a 'large rather than medium stature'. In the 1460s, and now in his thirties, the sultan is noted as having suffered from 'morbid corpulence' and 'inherited gout'.[67]

A compelling account made a decade later, in the 1470s, by Giovanni-Maria Angiolello (c.1451 - c.1525), an Italian from Vicenza, captive in the Ottoman service as a courtier, refers to Mehmet, now in his mid-forties, as 'fat and fleshy'. He further remarks upon the sultan's medium height and wide forehead, large eyes and thick lashes, as well as his aquiline nose, red beard, small mouth, short, thick neck and a sallow complexion. The totality of Angiolello's observations, which also include a reference to Mehmet's 'loud voice', convey a palpable sense of fascination in his Ottoman host.[68]

Opinion will naturally vary from one eye-witness account to another, but the various portraits of Mehmet, coupled with those respective observations, as well as other corroborative evidence, leave no doubt that his physical form had changed considerably from young adulthood to middle age. This is clearly evident in a direct comparison between the *Magnus Princeps* portrait and that produced by Costanzo, elements of which reflect Angiolello's observations (figs. 18.1 and 18.2).

A sense of self-aggrandizement provides a further means of considering the chronology of the bronze relief, for which the fall of Constantinople represents the most telling point of reference. Casting its influence upon many spheres of Ottoman political and cultural life, it had enabled Mehmet, twenty-one years old and now sultan and emperor, to be addressed with an imperial detachment in keeping with his position as conqueror.[69] Titular references to the Great Prince and Great Emir may have been appropriate during a period of subdued political influence in the late 1440s or early 1450s, prior to or immediately following his father Murad's death in 1451, but such titles would hardly seem adequate for the heir to the East Roman Empire.

The very absence of imperial recognition on the bronze relief, coupled with a reverse without any design, would seem to reflect the absence of any notable achievement at the time of its commission. In that respect, as well as in others, it stands in marked contrast with the post-conquest medals by Costanzo, Bellini and Bertoldo (figs. 4, 6, 7). Yet another comparison may perhaps be drawn between the Latin titulature on the afore-mentioned Ottoman treaty with Venice in 1446 and a similar document concluded with La Serenissima in 1479, upon which Mehmet is now imperially addressed.[70]

Mehmet's period as a provincial governor or emir in Manisa in the mid- to late 1440s, when he may have attempted

18.1 (detail of 1)   18.2 (detail of 4)

to set up a government of his own, can be seen to represent a *terminus post quem* for the commission of the bronze relief.[71] The fall of Constantinople, seven years later, is thought to represent its *terminus ante quem.* In the middle of which, Mehmet's accession as sultan in 1451, at the age of nineteen, had placed him in a position of supreme power, now able to proclaim success 'over brothers and rivals'.[72] Against this political landscape, and in consideration of a portrait that could be of someone in their late teenaged years or their early twenties, the commission of the *Magnus Princeps* bronze relief can be placed either side of 1450.

• • • • •

The earliest evidence of an imperial studio of artists at the Ottoman court is believed to date to the 1480s. This was for painted portraits, rather than those modelled in relief. A notable feature of this imagery, in comparison with the work of

Western artists or those schooled in such traditions, is an absence of perspective.[73]

With no evidence in the 1440s and 1450s of artists at the Ottoman court – or elsewhere in the Islamic East – capable of producing a modelled relief portrait, the hand behind the *Magnus Princeps* relief points to a Western origin, with such skills to be found, for example, at long-established workshops and studios in Italy. Mehmet's expressively rendered features leave no doubt that they had been taken from life. The sense of immediacy, in the modelling of the portrait, draws a clear connection between the hand responsible for the initial sketches and the preparation of the wax model, from which the casting in bronze will have been taken.

The strongly characterized portrait of Mehmet and its fineness of line and expressive, low relief modelling, share the same subtleties with that of Pisanello's signed work.[74] Other considerations, including the absence of a signature and notable inconsistencies in the shape and form of the lettering, serve to rule out the master's involvement. As a pupil or follower of Pisanello, and with somewhat similar characteristics in style, Matteo de' Pasti can also be excluded as the artist responsible for this work.[75]

The *Magnus Princeps* relief has been loosely linked to the artists Pietro da Milano (c.1410-1473) and Francesco Laurana (c.1430-1502) and their brief interlude in the 1460s at the French court of René d'Anjou (1409-1480). The chronology would itself exclude such a connection, while the stylistic associations are themselves far from conclusive.[76] Both artists had distinguished careers as sculptors in their own right, whose respective working lives can be largely defined by a twenty-year age difference. That of Francesco was to flower in the late 1460s and 1470s; while from the 1430s Pietro enjoyed some twenty-five years as an increasingly celebrated sculptor of ornamental and figurative reliefs, formerly in Ragusa, and subsequently in Naples.[77]

Ragusa was a significant geographic intermediary between the Ottoman Empire and Naples, providing open and friendly channels of communication, with artists frequently migrating between the two. With commissions coming from patricians and rich merchants, the tribute-paying city-state was supplying clients with books, silverware and a variety of fine objects.[78] Illustrating that link, as well as the ability of its workshops to produce medallic portraits – though bearing no stylistic connection with the bronze relief of Mehmet – is a medal of King Alfonso V of Aragon (1396-1458), signed *Opus Pauli De Ragvsio* (the work of Paul of

Ragusa) and believed to have been made around 1450.[79]

Pietro da Milano's growing status as a sculptor was such that it brought him a commission from Alfonso V, in the early 1450s, as director of the triumphal arch of the Castel Nuovo in Naples. This was one of the great architectural schemes of its day and certainly the largest such undertaking in Italy, for which Alfonso had been 'simultaneously pleading' for the services of the great Italian sculptor Donatello (c.1386-1466). It is an indication of the 'substantial fame' that was now being enjoyed by Pietro, who was to establish his own workshop in Naples at this time.[80] His increasing celebrity as a sculptor of statuary and other figural work makes it no less likely that he would have joined Pisanello's workshop and been 'directed' by him, as has been suggested.[81]

Although there is no evidence linking Pietro da Milano to medallic work at this time, his earlier circumstances draw a possible Ottoman association with the much-travelled antiquary and epigraphist Cyriacos of Ancona (c.1391 - c.1452), who had a particular interest in Roman imperial iconography. Cyriacos had been advising Pietro on elements of form and lettering while the sculptor was working on a prominent civic project in Ragusa in the early 1440s.[82] It was an association brought about by Cyriacos's ardent pursuit of the classical past, having helped devise, for example, the Roman medallic portraits by the architect, sculptor and writer, Filarete (Antonio di Petro Averlino) (1400-1469) in the late 1430s or early 1440s.[83] Within this interconnected world, Cyriacos had attended the Council of Ferrara in 1438, where Pisanello's medal of John VIII had been conceived (fig. 2).

Cyriacos was known throughout the Eastern Mediterranean, being 'particularly esteemed among the Turks' at this time. A document signed by Murad II provided him with safe passage throughout Ottoman towns and localities, 'as if he were one of the sultan's own household'.[84]

With an appropriate go-between linking a Western artist with the Ottoman court, one might imagine the circumstances in which Cyriacos – aware of Ottoman imperial aspirations and those of Mehmet himself – was to produce specimens of recently made medals by Pisanello and others during his visit to Murad's court in the mid-1440s. By so doing, Cyriacos would not only help embody such Ottoman pretensions, but satisfy his own interests in propagating the Roman imperial model. Although there is no evidence to unify unequivocally the stylistc attributes of the *Magnus Princeps* relief with any specific artist, these associations provide the circumstances in which the very idea for such a project might have been conceived.

In the early 1450s Cyriacos was having discussions with Alfonso V, in relation to his grand architectural project and the exchange of artists between Ragusa and Naples.[85] Alfonso himself was an admirer of the medallic form, having been represented on several medals by Pisanello and members of his workshop as recently as 1449.[86]

The vast majority of medallic work in the 1440s and 1450s had been commissioned by patrons on the Italian peninsula, where the various aspects of production, including casting, finishing and patination would have taken place at studios and workshops in relative proximity.

Our present understanding of medal-making, and the movement of artists and workshops in the mid-fifteenth century, is insufficient to rule out the possibility that the entire work on the *Magnus Princeps* relief may have been carried out at the Ottoman capital of Edirne, by an artist yet to be identified. It would have avoided round trips of some sixteen hundred miles to workshops in Italy, while further enabling any additional adjustments to the wax model and the overall design, as might have been desired by Mehmet,

to be carried out without undue delay. Naples was to remain a significant focal point for artists, from where, some twenty years later, Costanzo would travel to the Ottoman court to take his medallic portrait of Mehmet, who had requested an artist with a 'high reputation' (fig. 4).[87]

• • • • •

Mehmet's desire to sit before different Western artists at various times of his life provides a rare opportunity in the fifteenth century to consider the veracity of the *Magnus Princeps* portrait as a faithful record of its subject. Though separated by some twenty-five years or more, its facial characteristics can be linked to the medallic portraits by Costanzo, Bertoldo and Bellini (figs. 4, 6, 7). It is, however, the thin face and distinctive nose on Gentile Bellini's painted portrait in oil, taken within a year or so of Mehmet's death, which most closely reflect the physiognomy of the youth on the bronze relief (figs. 19.1-19.2).[88] With respective portraits taken from opposite ends of his adult life and in different genres, such a conclusion is particularly telling, and further concurs with Angiolello's observation of Mehmet. A comparison between these two portraits and those of Mehmet's great-grandson, Suleyman the Magnificent (r.1520-1566), notably align

19.1 (detail of 1)

19.2 (detail of 5)

20.1

20.2

20.1. Venetian, workshop or circle of Gentile Bellini: *Suleyman the Magnificent, c.*1520, oil on panel, 28 x 32.5 cm., detail (courtesy of Sotheby's, 2021); 20.2. Venetian, workshop or circle of Titian: *Suleyman the Magnificent, c.*1535, oil on canvas, 85 x 99 cm., detail (Kunst Historisches Museum, Vienna, Gemäldegalerie; # 2429*).

several of these characteristics, suggesting them to be genetic (figs.19.1–19.2; 20.1–20.2).

The vibrant characterization of the *Magnus Princeps* portrait would seem to reflect a natural fascination by the artist in Mehmet, who may well be the first fully identifiable Muslim subject to be represented in bronze relief. There is the sense of a cold detachment, which resonates with eye-witness accounts of the young sultan: peering absently into the distance, possessed of a melancholy nature, laughing seldom and full of circumspection.[89] Costanzo's more mature portrait does little to dispel such conclusions (fig. 18.2).

The clearly defined characteristics of the *Magnus Princeps* portrait draw an uneasy comparison with a medal purporting to carry a representation of Mehmet, who is referred to in its heavily blundered legend as 'Macomet' (fig. 21). With orientalised features that veer between caricature and stereotype and an uncertain chronology, the portrait is devoid of any elements that can be physically linked to the sultan; nor can the cap, turban and clothing be associated with authentic Ottoman dress.[90] Hampered by the absence of a reliable sketch, the artist attempted, nonetheless, to provide a representation of Mehmet.

Failings of quite a different kind reveal themselves in a portrait medal produced a century or more after Mehmet's death, of which a number of specimens were cast in

21. Unidentified artist: unknown portrait, *c*.1460-70, cast bronze medal, 61 mm.
(Ashmolean Museum, Oxford: Heberden Coin Room, HCR 9472).

bronze and silver (fig. 22).[91] It is believed to have been based on a surviving sketch of the original composition, as might be concluded from the accurate rendering of Mehmet's titulature. However, the portrait is notable for its disconcerting grimace, while a further departure from the original composition is an absence of calligraphic patterning and decoration in the sultan's woven cap. A design and inscription have been introduced on the reverse, which features the heads of three eagles in the centre and a surrounding legend in French: IEHAN TRIEAVDET DE SELONGEY A FEYT FAIRE CESTE PIECE (Jean Tricaudet of Selongey made this piece).

Believed on stylistic criteria to have been produced in the sixteenth or seventeenth century, the circumstances in which 'Jean Tricaudet' had come to make this medal are yet to be known. An anomaly of the eight or more extant specimens are variable diameters and surfaces that have all been harshly tooled and chased.[92]

22. Unidentified artist: '*Tricaudet' portrait*, c.1600-1700, cast bronze medal, 84 mm.
(F.R. Kunker, Osnabrück; Auction 289, 14 March 2017, Lot 1509).

3

IMAGE AND PROTECTION

Sufficiently skilled though the artist was in creating the *Magnus Princeps* portrait, its components ultimately reflect the manner with which Mehmet chose to be represented. This might be seen, for example, not only in his choice of patterned kaftan, but by the inclusion of a feather that projects somewhat incongruously from the rear of his lace cap. This feature may be no more than a decorative addition to the ensemble, but the allusion to flight might also be a nod to his great-grandfather, Bayezid I, widely referred to as *Yildirim*, or Thunderbolt, for the rapidity with which he moved his Ottoman troops.

Having played a significant part in enlarging Ottoman domain in the 1390s, Bayezid's influence upon his successors is evident, with Mehmet having named his first-born son Bayezid II in 1447. In many ways Bayezid had anticipated the centralizing vision of Mehmet, who continued to pay tribute to his great-

grandfather over the following twenty-five years in one form or another, assuming for himself the title of 'Thunderbolt' on his medal by Costanzo (fig. 4).

The influence of Alexander the Great (d. 323 B.C.) was to play its own part in Mehmet's upbringing, finding symbolic representation in an illustrated history of the *Iskendername* or 'Alexander Romance'. It includes images of the feather on the headgear of figures that also appear in painted Islamic miniatures. Alongside texts produced by the historical poet, writer and Ottoman versifier, Ahmedi (1330-1413), written around 1402 as a contemporary epic, these Alexander romances sought to establish a historical context and identity for the Ottomans.[93]

For the ambitious and imperially envisioned Ottoman heir, the medallic form represented a more sophisticated and meaningful level of representation than the coinage struck in the names of

opposite
23. Pisanello: *Lodovico II Gonzaga, 2nd Marquess of Mantua*, c.1447-1448, cast bronze medal, 100 mm. (National Gallery of Art, Washington, D.C.; Samuel H. Kress Collection, # 1957.14.608).

Alexander the Great and Constantine the Great, or indeed those struck in Mehmet's own name. This demonstration of an artist's skill, in undulating relief and cast bronze, projected a clear and unequivocal sense of identity.

The concept of Holy War or ghaza (sometimes gaza) was a major contributing factor in the foundation and development of the Ottoman state, to which many ambitious emirates within Islam aspired for the purposes of enlarging territory. It represented a commonplace ethos in the 1300s and 1400s that blended the search for booty or pasture with political opportunism and religious motivation, having evolved from earlier and less refined origins. In attempting to provide a history for the Ottomans, Ahmedi sought to explain or rationalize the role of the ghazi as an instrument of the religion of Allah, being both a 'servant of God' and a 'sword of God'. It was with such beliefs that the Ottoman hunger for empire came to represent an enduring territorial struggle against their Christian neighbours, but it also extended to major conquests in the Muslim world.[94]

With a phenomenon that was not limited to either place or culture, there was little in principle to separate the ghazi chivalry of Mehmet and his contemporaries and the refined chivalric orders evolving in Europe and elsewhere in the wake of the Crusades. Some sense of that tradition, honour and respect is evoked by a latter-day commentary on the Ottoman victory at Nicopolis in 1396, when Bayezid I is described as having engaged with a crusader army of Europe's 'proudest knights'.[95]

Mehmet's vision of himself as a present-day Alexander sat side by side with that of a ghazi warrior of the faith. No longer the feared and despised adventurers that they were centuries earlier, the ghazi at their higher and more sophisticated echelons had become noble knights, among the ranks of whom an Ottoman sultan or an Italian prince would wish to take their respective place.

Many of the medals being made by Pisanello in the 1440s provide a striking visual representation of the genre, in which powerful rulers of Italian city-states, resplendent in chivalric garb, extravagantly embraced such values. Patrons of the artist, such as Sigismondo Malatesta (fig. 14) and Lodovico II Gonzaga of Mantua (1412-1478) (fig. 23), are amongst those who illustrate that desire for warrior symbolism.[96] In the light of Mehmet's own aspirations, it becomes understandable just how influential the potency of that imagery must have been upon the adolescent Ottoman prince.

Medals could also carry more subtle imagery, such as that by Pisanello of Leonello d'Este, Marquis of Ferrara (1407-1450) (fig. 24). Produced around 1442, it presents the subject as a modern day Alexander, with an allegorical reverse suggesting the means by which Leonello could emulate or indeed rival the great empire-builder.[97] There was little separating such universal ambitions from those to which Mehmet himself could be associated. This is suggested by the reclining figure on the anonymous bronze medal, referred to earlier (fig. 21), which recalls the reverse of Pisanello's medal of Leonello.

• • • • •

Mehmet's formal representation on the bronze relief conveys a sense of occasion that will surely have been as remarkable for the subject as it would have been for the Western artist engaged in taking this portrait. However it is to be explained, the prominent exposed area to the rear

24. Pisanello: *Leonello d'Este, Marquis of Ferrara*, c.1442, cast bronze medal, 79 mm. (National Gallery of Art, Washington D.C.; Samuel H. Kress Collection, # 1957.14.601).

of Mehmet's head is a clear departure from his other portraits, on all of which the turban can be seen to cover his entire head (figs. 25.1-25.5). A similarly exposed area on Pisanello's medal of Filippo Maria Visconti has been explained as a prevailing fashion (fig. 3).[98]

These personal preferences are also reflected in other ways, such as the direction in which Mehmet's portrait was to face. In the context of universal ambition and the Ottoman march West, this can be seen as an unwavering commitment to conquest. That sense of determination, and the need for its affirmation, will have been reinforced by the earlier failures of Mehmet's father and great-grandfather to take Constantinople. It was a message that would continue to be picked up across the Eastern Mediterranean. Nervously reflecting on the young sultan's intentions, following the fall of the Byzantine capital, Cardinal Bessarion had been in no doubt as to Mehmet's unbending desire of 'reversing the eastward march of Western rulers', warning of the dangers now threatening Italy, not to mention other lands.[99]

The importance to Mehmet of imagery and symbolism is notable on the medal commissioned in the mid-1470s from Costanzo, who has been referred to as an 'intelligent appreciator' of Pisanello's great

25.1 (detail of 1)

25.2 (detail of 4)

25.3 (detail of 5)

25.4 (detail of 7)

25.5 (detail of 8)

qualities (fig. 4).[100] Many artists copied his designs, but in this instance the equestrian figure, taken from the master's medal of John VIII, has been reversed by Costanzo from right to left (figs. 26.1-26.2). There is no logical reason why the artist would have changed a ready-made design in such a radical way. As such, it would seem to reflect the symbolic importance placed by Mehmet upon such matters and the sense of an 'uncompromising nature' and 'absolutist vision', which were amongst the characteristics most clearly remembered after his death.[101]

It aligns with Costanzo's representation of Mehmet on the obverse of this medal, which conveys a confidence perfectly in keeping with that of a conqueror. The diameter of the medal itself, far exceeding that of almost every other Renaissance medal, can also be seen as an expression of power.

Recalling the memory of Mehmet's great-grandfather, *Yildirim* Bayezid, and the thunderbolt of war – HIC BELLVM FVLMEN – this modern-day Alexander had felt justified in claiming his illustrious forebear's title for himself; having not only succeeded in bringing about the fall of the Byzantine capital at such a young age, but being well on the way to creating a world empire.[102] Mehmet's own chronicler, Kritovoulos (c.1410-c.1470),

26.1 (detail of 2)

26.2 (detail of 4)

would similarly refer to the sultan as a thunderbolt, 'burning, ruining and destroying everything'.[103]

• • • • •

The modelled relief portrait may have been a Western concept, but in Mehmet's pursuit of imperial supremacy it was also to prove an ideal vehicle for integrating elements culturally closer to home. Among the more conspicuous aspects of his own heritage was that of calligraphic script, which over many centuries constituted a fundamental element of Islamic art. Its enduring decorative character has provided designers, illuminators and bookbinders, and others involved in the arts, with creative opportunities.[104] A relatively early example, from the fourteenth century, is a Persian Qur'an stand in teak, a panel of which elegantly incorporates the frequently cited opening words of the Qur'an, the bismillah, 'In the name of God, in the name of Allah, the merciful, the compassionate' (fig. 27).[105]

This ubiquitous acclamation has been represented over centuries in various calligraphic forms. With styles of script differing from one school to another, such skills came to be practised and developed on all manner of decorative arts, including coins, jewellery, textiles, weapons and armour.[106] With an increasingly wide use of calligraphic texts and pictures, or calligrams, the greatest masters of the craft were able to assimilate design and form with considerable ingenuity, in what was seen as both an artistic and intellectual pursuit. Some practitioners in the 'art of the word' attempted to present knowledge through writing, while artists preferring the 'art of the form' strove to depict the world around them by means of the picture. While calligraphy and painting may have been considered two discrete methods of communication, each revealing imaginative and creative skills, they occasionally merged in a form of 'creative synthesis'.[107]

Surviving examples of this phenomenon from the fifteenth century are rare, but an Ottoman scroll, dating to 1458, works 'to associate' Mehmet with God in its benediction of the sultan's kingdom, its complex form having illustrated one of the earliest surviving examples of zoomorphic calligraphy. In this particular instance the figures of a bird and lion are rendered in a script that deliberately plays on the inherent ambiguity between text and image, meaning and form.[108]

The Anatolian, Şeyh Hamdullah (1436–1520), along with his 'mystical visions', has been identified as the originator of calligraphic art within the Ottoman tradition, from whom can be

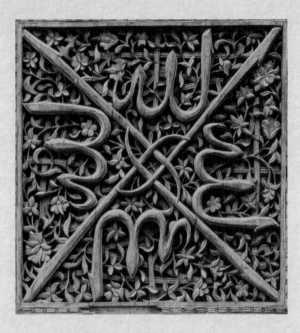

27. *An upright panel from a teak Persian Qur'anic prayer stand* (detail), *c*.1360;
attributed to Hasan [ibn] Zain ibn Sulaiman al-Isfahani, 114 cm. x 127 cm. x 42 cm.
(Metropolitan Museum of Art, New York; Rogers, 1910, # 10.218)

28 (detail of 1)

traced an unbroken chain of transmission from master to disciple.[109] Practitioners of the craft were highly esteemed and would be patronised by successive Ottoman sultans, some of whom became accomplished calligraphers in their own right – Mehmet's son, Bayezid II, having been tutored by Şeyh Hamdullah.[110]

The art of calligraphy was to develop over the centuries into more commonly found pictorial forms. Integrating flair and ingenuity in its mode of expression, this could represent, for example, an early seventeenth century composition of a peacock. The practice of weaving an inscription into the form of an animal, bird, flower, or an inanimate object such as a ship, remains a popular *tour de force* among Islamic calligraphers to this day.[111]

Creative synthesis of another kind appears to be present on the *Magnus Princeps* bronze relief, which has integrated, in a cursive script, the Arabic phrase *li-llah* - 'To God' or 'For God' - within the decorative pattern of Mehmet's woven cap (fig. 28).[112] With writing being a natural transmission of thought to paper, the presence of this feature, directly above the sultan's head, can be seen as a metaphor for that process. The design for the bronze relief will have been a collaboration between artist and sitter, providing Mehmet with

an opportunity of projecting himself as a receptor of Allah's Divine message and a servant of God. While this is a speculative interpretation, it concurs with someone who saw himself as the inheritor of Constantine the Great's legacy and an iconography that is unmistakably imperial in content. With prophecies foretelling an event widely regarded as 'the work of Allah' and a 'miracle of His Providence', the fall of Constantinople constituted an overarching imperative, going back centuries, with premonitory texts exercising an enduring influence.[113]

•   •   •   •   •

Beyond the symbolic relevance of the *Magnus Princeps* bronze relief, though not entirely detached from it, is the practical role that it may have served for Mehmet as a form of talisman or amulet. The meticulously prepared piercing and the blank reverse are amongst the features to raise the question, while Bertoldo's portrait of the sultan, depicting a pendant-like object suspended from his neck, similarly suggests it to warrant consideration (fig. 29).

It would be far from being the only occasion in which the medallic form would find deployment as a talisman, which provided protection and prophetic blessing for both viewer and user, when held or worn in proximity to the body.[114] The talisman is represented by a bewildering variety of forms and types and has a convoluted history, within Islam, that goes back to the eighth century.[115] The most significant component of its 'magical vocabulary' was the Qur'an itself, with its invocations to a revered figure such as the Prophet Muhammad and his 'ability to perform miracles', as conspicuously realized on the afore-mentioned Persian prayer stand (fig. 27). The presence of Qur'anic symbols and texts, and in particular the bismillah, were thus believed able to promote an object's protective qualities, addressed as such evocations generally were to 'God or one of His intercessors'.[116]

Ranging hugely in type and form, amongst such talismans that can be directly associated with the Ottoman court is a 'magic square' that a grand vizier used to protect himself.[117] Of more intricate nature is a 100 cm. talismanic sword decorated with protective inscriptions, being one of three provenanced to Mehmet himself (fig. 30).[118] Amongst the most conspicuous and stylistically consistent examples of the genre is the talismanic shirt, which would be adorned with Qur'anic verses and prayers, letters and numerological equivalents; these having been 'demanded regularly' by members of the Ottoman dynasty 'eager to benefit from their military and political application'.[119] An example of such a shirt is that attributed to Cem (1459-1495), another of Mehmet's sons (fig. 31).[120]

Mehmet's use of the talisman concurs with a belief 'in visions of the unknown' and the 'divine signs' observed during the siege of Constantinople; upon which his mystic, spiritual guide and physician, Sheikh Akşemseddin (d. 1459) would pronounce.[121] A modern-day analysis of

29 (detail of 7)

the six-week siege suggests that Mehmet's personal preparations for the final assault on the Byzantine capital would, 'in all likelihood', have included the donning of a talismanic shirt, richly embroidered with verses from the Qur'an and the names of God.[122] There is no evidence to support the hypothesis, yet seen in the light of this prevailing culture and Mehmet's personality, it becomes perfectly plausible. After all, the vast array of talismanic material associated with the Ottoman court and offering 'intimacy' to God, had clearly been made for the purpose of wearing 'near or against the owner's body'.[123] While the wider significance of Constantinople for Mehmet and the Ottoman enterprise would have created its own sense of urgency.

Objects patently military in application, such as a Turkish field ensign, would carry Qur'anic verses that requested 'Help from God and early victory'.[124] Similar in nature is a seventeenth-century Ottoman banner staff-head (fig. 32). This has been inscribed with the Shahada, a profession of faith, proclaiming that 'There is no god but God, and Muhammad is the messenger of God'.

30. Unknown Ottoman maker: *talismanic sword of Mehmet II*, second half of the fifteenth century, steel, salmon teeth and iron, 100 cm. (The Presidency of the Republic of Turkey, Directorate of National Palaces Administration, Topkapi Palace Museum, Istanbul; # TSM 1/375).

The full extent of this material provides evidence of an occultist renaissance in the 1400s.[125] It would remain a mainstream cultural force, with no limitations as to what shape or form a talisman was to take. This industry grew exponentially in the mid-fifteenth century, with a library inventory taken under the reign of Bayezid II in 1503 providing some idea of its extent at the Ottoman court. Amongst the materials listed are 'chests full of inscribed artefacts: talismanic shirts, skull caps, amulets and tablets made of wood, copper, and silver'; with some 208 recorded items offering 'a glimpse into the supplicatory, devotional, and talismanic practices'.[126]

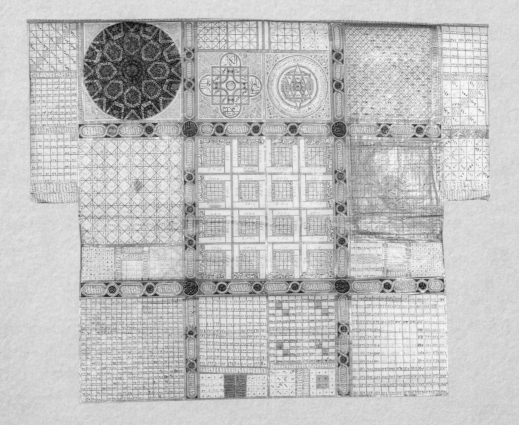

31. Unknown Ottoman maker: *talismanic shirt attributed to the ownership of Cem, Mehmet II's son*, 113 cm. in width, and 120 cm. in length; and indicating the commencement of making on 30 March 1477 and completion on 29 March 1480. (The Presidency of the Republic of Turkey, Directorate of National Palaces Administration, Topkapi Palace Museum, Istanbul; # TSM 13/1404).

Being of a handy-sized format and easily wearable, a medallic portrait was the perfect host for the integration of symbolism, metaphor and universal triumph. It provided as much opportunity for an artist to 'conjure up living beings' as one working with oil, brush and canvas.[127] At an Ottoman court populated by mystic lettrists, Arabic stylists, and skilled calligraphers, divinatory science had become thoroughly embedded in political and courtly life, as would the opportunity for its novel integration.[128]

The *Magnus Princeps* bronze relief represents a private commission by Mehmet, intended solely for his own edification, in whatever form that may have taken. In that respect, it is little different to the medal he would commission from Costanzo, some twenty years later, in the 1470s (fig. 4).[129]

32. Unknown Ottoman maker: *Turkish Banner staff head*, c.1675-1700, gilt-bronze, 17.8 cm. in width, and 54.9 cm. in length (Metropolitan Museum of Art, New York; bequest of George C. Stone, 1935, # 36.25.2861).

4

DESTINY AND TRIUMPH

Following the death of Bayezid I in 1402 and a prolongued civil war, the Ottomans were able to re-establish their former positions in Rumelia and Anatolia after the accession of Mehmet I in 1413. The failure by Bayezid to provide adequately for the succession had endorsed the need to legitimize the many claims that would be made by various Ottoman factions over subsequent decades. The transition from an oral to a written culture, with texts and illustrated histories, was to help address that crisis of identity with a clearer sense of historical consciousness.[130]

It reinforced the need for Murad II to ensure that the line of succession would reside in the most capable hands, strong enough to withstand a contested leadership struggle. The Ottoman victory against the Hungarians at Varna in November 1444 proved sufficient in its significance to raise their profile further.

The roles of regent and sultan fell easily on Mehmet, while his position as a provincial governor or emir in Manisa in the late 1440s had done little to suppress those ambitions. By the time of Murad II's death in 1451, the family's political structure was believed strong enough to enable the nineteen year-old, and his military advisers, to revive the vision of empire set out by his great-grandfather, *Yildirim* Bayezid, sixty years earlier.[131]

Murad II's death was an occasion greeted by the Byzantines and many in the West with a sense of relief, having been on the Ottoman throne for almost thirty years. However, for those who knew better, it would prove a moment of caution. George Sphrantzes (1400-1477), the trusted ambassador of Constantine XI (1405-1453) – son and successor of Emperor John VIII – was crossing the Black Sea on a diplomatic mission, unaware of the passing of Murad. Arriving at Trebizond, John IV Komnenos (r. 1429-1458), emperor of that territory, greeted him jovially with the news, little realizing that for Sphrantzes, and for many others already familiar with the ambitious Ottoman heir, these were far from glad tidings.[132]

As Mehmet put his campaign for Constantinople into operation, a natural sense of tactical cunning was to embrace such gambits as the negotiation of treaties with the West and the rapid construction of a strategically positioned fortress on the Bosphorus. In so doing, Mehmet had effectively cut Constantinople off from the help of its Western allies, prior to laying siege to the capital in early April 1453. Requiring a force believed to have been upwards of 60,000 strong, along with a similar-sized logistical back-up, the Ottoman campaign would successfully conclude almost two months later on 29 May. Among the more audacious features of this frequently retold episode was the overland transportation of galleys from the Bosphorus shore down into the Golden Horn, in order to avoid a chained link defence running across its mouth. The Ottomans were also to construct a pontoon bridge across the harbour from Galata to Constantinople, enabling their forces to attack the walls on that side of the city, while throughout deploying the latest siege and cannon technology. As his chronicler Kritovoulos would remark, the taking of Constantinople was an enterprise upon which Mehmet had 'long since elaborated'.[133]

Prepared by Helen Stirling

As both sultan and emperor, victory had enabled Mehmet to settle, in earnest, the pressing issue relating to Ottoman succession. Hostage-taking had been a ploy consistently used over decades by the Byzantines against previous Ottoman sultans. It was to re-emerge once again, with Constantine XI demanding increased payments for the upkeep of a second cousin and potential Ottoman claimant called Orhan. It was for such purpose that the legislation of fratricide had been intended, eliminating all tendencies towards dynastic fragmentation. Sufficiently empowered, Mehmet was to deal with such threats in an uncompromising and conclusive fashion, having sought out Orhan and any sons that his father may have sired from his harem, as well as those from any of his wives.[134]

Mehmet was also in a position to break free from the traditional pattern of power sharing that had long existed between the Ottoman dynasty and the Turkish warrior nobility. An inevitable consequence was the fate to befall Halil Pasha, Murad's Grand Vizier. Held responsible by Mehmet for his relegated role as a provincial governor, following a pre-emptive attempt on Constantinople in 1446, Halil Pasha was arrested, charged with treason and executed.[135]

Murad II had recognized in the teenaged Mehmet the resolve and determination necessary to expand the empire, which such decisive acts had now confirmed. Those characteristics were to assume a more mature physical realisation twenty-five years later on Costanzo's medal of Mehmet: the fullness of the neck suggesting the strength of a bull and a savage temper, with watchful eyes that reflect rapacity (fig. 4).[136]

• • • • •

Images of the antique triumph, on paintings and sculpture, provided Renaissance rulers and other patrons of the arts with the means of linking their visual persona and achievements to the success associated with imperial Rome. The advent of the medallic portrait in the 1430s had provided a further means by which to manipulate the 'eloquent expression' and ambitions of such patrons, with an iconography that owed much to Roman imperial coinage.[137]

In furtherance of such associations, Leon Battista Alberti (1401-1472), the architect, cartographer, painter and sculptor, had appropriated the medallic portrait in the mid-1430s for a representation of himself (fig. 33). Taking a particularly large and distinctive oval format, he had incorporated the device of a winged human eye alongside his portrait,

33.   Leon Battista Alberti: *Self-portrait*, c.1435, cast bronze relief, 136 x 201 mm. (reverse plain)
(National Gallery of Art Washington, D.C.; Samuel H. Kress Collection, # 1957.14.125).

suggesting the means by which the entire universe would become visible. By so doing, Alberti had aligned himself with the greatest emperors.[138] He may have exemplified the 'Renaissance Man', in his broad range of interests and aspirations, but a growing number of contemporaries were to reflect their own ambitions and cultural tastes in this manner. Sigismondo Malatesta had been a particularly prolific devotee (figs. 14-15), as was his brother, Domenico Novello Malatesta, Lord Cesena and Cervia (1418-1465). Having commissioned a medal from Pisanello in the mid-1440s, Domenico is presented kneeling before a crucifix, fully armoured (fig. 34).[139] In keeping with the interests of such patrons, he was also a collector of books and in communication with writers, historians, humanists and scholars.[140]

Ottoman coinage had a place for an aspiring political entity in its early years of formation, but the innovation of medallic portraiture, a century later, was to present a more imaginative and compelling opportunity for Mehmet, as it was already

34. Pisanello: *Domenico Malatesta, Lord of Cesena and Cervia*, c.1445-1448, cast bronze medal, 86 mm. (National Gallery of Art Washington, D.C.; Samuel H. Kress Collection, # 1957.14.607).

doing for others. Inculcated as heir to Murad II and the Ottoman sultanate, his far-sighted vision, as the inheritor of Constantine the Great's legacy, could now be embodied in this manner. With a formal representation of the subject in modelled bronze relief and an encircled titulature, the medallic portrait provided a sense of historical consciousness, which written and illustrated works were attempting to do more widely for the Ottomans.

Despite the general absence of relief portraiture within Islamic culture, the commission of the *Magnus Princeps* relief reflects Mehmet's willingness to patronize artists of merit, whoever they may be and regardless of their origins. It aligns with his desire of forging a broader East-West geopolitical identity, which was to be most publicly expressed in the rebuilding and repopulation of Constantinople, in the years following its fall in 1453.[141]

Mehmet's interest in medallic portraiture would not abate over the following two decades, although attempts to commission further representations did not always bear fruit. Writing to Sigismondo Malatesta in the early 1460s, and successfully requesting the services of his master-medallist, Matteo de' Pasti, the artist was arrested en route to Constantinople, in the belief that he was a spy, denying Mehmet a medal by that hand.[142]

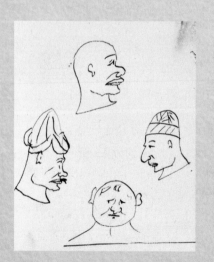 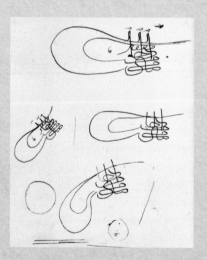

35. Artist unknown, but possibly Mehmet II:
35.1 *Drawings of Heads*, c.1445-1450, or later. 35.2 *Drawings of Mehmet's Tughra*, c.1445-1450, or later.
(The Presidency of the Republic of Turkey, Directorate of National Palaces Administration;
Topkapi Palace Museum, Istanbul; # H. 2324, fol. 44b).

In the light of this enduring interest, it would be little surprise to learn that medals of princely and other Italian contemporaries might also have resided amongst the books, prints and engravings in the Ottoman court library. One survivor from that period is an exercise or sketch book of sixty pages, some of them watermarked and dateable to 'about 1444', containing unsigned designs which have been linked to the hand of the young Mehmet.[143] Executed in black ink with a brush and reed pen, they include sketched portraits of rudimentary endeavour, three-dimensional in depiction, which clearly express a Western medallic influence (fig. 35.1). Providing a more direct association with the Ottoman prince are seven sketches that constitute his personal tughra or signature (fig. 35.2). Of unique authority, this calligraphic emblem would be included on official court documents, being neither easily read nor copied.

The circumstances in which the *Magnus Princeps* bronze relief was to leave the Ottoman court are not known, though it would be reasonable to conclude that this had occurred after Mehmet's death, in 1481, and possibly at much the same time as the departure of Costanzo's medal (fig. 4) and the Bellini oil (fig. 5). All three works were to re-emerge in the second half of the nineteenth century, the bronze relief

remaining in private ownership, while Costanzo's medal and the Bellini oil were to enter public collections.

• • • • •

As the stylistic breadth and chronology of Mehmet's portraiture confirms, his desire for a place in the pantheon of fame could be satisfied by both territorial acquisition and the preservation of his image. Unusual though this inclination and its practical realisation may have been for someone of the Muslim faith, the political backdrop to the sultan's teenaged years provides the clearest indication of a young man ready to place himself before a Western artist and a genre that offered imperial status and titular authority. An early commission had taken the form of the *Magnus Princeps* bronze relief, though not every attempt by Mehmet to have such a portrait was to prove successful.

That precocious ambition had been observed in its nascent form by Mehmet's father - and remarked upon, to his own cost, by his guardian, Halil Pasha - while the sense of an awe-inspiring conqueror was also to resonate beyond the confines of the Ottoman court, during his teenaged years.[144]

Murad II had been well placed to recognize the youthful determination and far-sightedness of his son, to whom he had handed the reins of power in 1444, though little could he have imagined that within a decade of confirming the line of succession, the gates of Constantinople would open to an Ottoman army with Mehmet the Conqueror at its head.

The Ottomans considered themselves the Romans of the Muslim world and the young sultan's rapid ascent, within its dynastic hierarchy, was to herald the most critical period in their evolution. Historically aware and aesthetically attuned, Mehmet's auspicious representation in bronze relief, as the much foretold, last Roman emperor, stands testament to the vision and self-belief that had made possible such a triumph.

NOTES

1. Christie's auction, Rome, 13-14 December, 2000, 'Monete, Medaglie, Decorazioni e Libri di Numismatica' Lot 696 ('Varie fusioni di scarsa qualità di Medaglie dal XV al XVII sec., (12), inc. Carlo Borromeo (2), Sultan Maometto, Cero Ferro, Maffeo Barberini, Francesco Zanotti'), purchased by the author. The auction contained several hundred lots of European Renaissance and later medals, many accompanied by hand-written inked tickets, square and circular. Though clearly coming from an old collection, no provenance was stated in the catalogue, nor subsequently provided by Christie's.

2. Spinale, p. 3, et seq.; Necipoğlu, p. 21. For the posthumous medal of Mehmet, see fig. 22. See below, Note 129.

3. Freely, p. 57. For details of Bessarion, with regard to his collecting interests, see Campbell, *Bellini and the East* (2005), 'The Bellini, Bessarion and Byzantium', pp. 36-63. Warnings of the Ottoman threat echoed widely, with the humanist scholar, Lauro Quirini, informing Pope Nicholas V how Mehmet saw himself as a new Alexander the Great (Pertusi, p. 80).

4. Babinger, p. 11. There is debate amongst certain scholars about Mehmet's year of birth, with some sources stating it to be 1430 rather than 1432 (cf. Wittek/Heywood, p. 163). The two-year discrepancy has little bearing on the conclusions reached in this present study, which bases its calculations on the year of 1432.

5. Inalcik, p. 59; and Kafadar, p. 137.

6. For example, Rogers, *Bellini and the East*, p. 80; Inalcik (2000), p. 181; and Necipoğlu, Notes 27-32.

7. Judith Pfeiffer, 'The Ottoman Muse Flattered, but Poorly Winged: Müeyyedzade, Bayezid II, and the Early Sixteenth-Century Ottoman Literary Canon', *Treasures of Knowledge* (2019), pp. 241-266.

8. Rogers, *Bellini and the East*, pp. 81-83; while for other aspects of Mehmet's collecting interests, see Raby, 'Sultan of Paradox' (1982) and 'Greek Scriptorium' (1983); as well as 'East and West in Mehmed the Conqueror's Library', *Bulletin du Bibliophile 3* (1987) pp. 297-318.

9. Raby and Tanindi, p. 62.

10. For an inventory and other elements of Bayezid II's library, see *Treasures of Knowledge*, Vol. 1.

11. John Cunnally, *The Role of Greek and Roman Coins in the Art of the Italian Renaissance* (University of Pennsylvania, 1984); and Vermeule, pp. 261 et passim. For a discussion of classical learning and medallic art, see Scher (1994), pp. 15-16.

12. For the processes of medal making in the Italian Renaissance, see for example Scher (1994), pp.13-14; and Pollard xv-xviii. For aspects of form and convention, see Syson and Gordon, 'Classical Learning and Court Art', pp. 86-137.

13. Hill, pp. 6-13; Kress, pp. 7-10; Pollard, pp. 2-18; Scher (1994), pp. 43-58; Scher (2019), pp. 38-44; Syson and Gordon, and Weiss.

14. Armand 1: 7, 20; *Bellini and the East*, fig. 26; Hill, 19; Kress, 1; Necipoğlu, fig. 2; Pollard, 1; Raby (1987), fig. 2; Scher (1994), 4; Scher (2019), 1; Syson and Gordon, fig 1.35; Waddington, pp. 6-8; and Weiss.

15. Armand 1:8, 23; Hill 21; Kress 3; Pollard 2; Scher (2019), 2; Syson and Gordon, fig. 2.24.

16. By the time of his death in 1455, Pisanello had attracted more than twelve patrons to the medal. Hill's *Corpus* records 1204 medals, executed by more than 150 artists between the 1430s and the 1530s.

17. Armand, 1: 79, 2; Bellini and the East, p. 71; Hill, 321; Kress, 102; Necipoğlu,

fig. 17a; Pollard, 145; Raby (1987), fig. 5; Raby in Scher (1994), pp. 87-89, No. 21 (which provides some background to the movements and work of Costanzo); Waddington, p. 9. See below, Note 87.

18. Inscribed on the lower two corners: MCCCCLXXX / DIE XXV. ME (right-hand side) and / JL (?) ISQV. . .R/. . . OR ORBIS...CVNCTARE. (left-hand side, which is damaged). Though the Bellini oil of Mehmet was believed to have undergone significant and irreconcilable restoration in the nineteenth century, a recent examination has confirmed that much more of the portrait painted on 25 November 1480 survives than has been sometimes supposed: Campbell, *Bellini and the East*, pp. 78-79; Necipoğlu, fig. 18. See also, Elizabeth Rodini, 'The sultan's true face? Gentile Bellini, Mehmet II, and the values of verisimilitude', in *The Turk and Islam in the Western Eye 1450-1470* (2016), ed. James G. Harper, at pp. 21-40; and *Gentile Bellini's Portrait of Sultan Mehmed II: Lives and Afterlives of an Iconic Image* (London, 2020).

19. Armand, I: 76; *Bellini and the East*, pp. 74-75; Hill, 432; Kress, 144; Necipoğlu, fig. 17d; Pollard, 165; Raby (1987), fig. 7. There is a variant on some specimens of the medal that omits the letter 'F' between 'Sultani' and 'Mohameti' as well as the

floriate decoration to the otherwise plain hem of the coat beneath Mehmet's kaftan.

20. Armand, 1: 78, 3; *Bellini and the East*, pp. 76-77; Hill, 911; Kress, 248; Necipoğlu, fig. 17c; Pollard, 282; Raby (1987), fig. 8; James David Draper, in Scher (1994), pp. 126-128, which provides an expansive commentary dealing with the iconography.

21. Rogers, *Bellini and the East*, pp. 88-89, fig. 34; Necipoğlu, fig. 19.

22. Rogers, *Bellini and the East*, pp. 88-89, fig. 35; Necipoğlu, fig. 20.

23. Armand, I, 78, 1; *Bellini and the East*, pp. 72-73; Hill, 322; Necipoğlu, fig. 17b; Raby (1987), fig. 6.

24. Amongst the many painted and other portraits assigned as being of Mehmet and contemporary to his lifetime, or produced shortly thereafter, is a gouache by an unknown Persian hand. Published by Sakisian, Plate II, D, and dated to c. 1460, the identification of the sitter is uncertain. There are medals produced in lead, likely to have been made after Mehmet's death, which carry portraits that do not appear to be factual representations (Hill 1203-1204). Similar portraits, purporting to be of Mehmet, and sometimes captioned *El Gran Turco*, occur on prints and ceramics that were produced before and after his death (*Bellini and the East*, figs. 27-28; Weiss, plates XV-XVI).

25. Kafadar, p. 61; Wittek, pp. 38-40, which presents a form of genetic analysis of Ottoman origins.

26. Kafadar, pp.134-146.

27. Inalcik, pp. 9-16.

28. Inalcik, p. 16; Wittek, p. 164.

29. Kastritsis, pp. 3, 37-38, 200.

30. Kafadar, p. 137.

31. Kafadar, p. 156.

32. Joseph Gill, *The Council of Florence* (Cambridge, 1959).

33. Pollard, figs 1 and 2; Syson and Gordon, pp. 29-34; Weiss, Plate IX.

34. The term 'Roman' was in common usage to describe the Greeks (Byzantines) of Constantinople, which was itself frequently referred to as the New Rome.

35. Nicol, p. 381. Weiss describes the distribution as 'plentiful', p. 19; while Raby suggests that the medal was 'known in the Levant' (1982), p. 4. For influences of this iconography, see for example, Joyce Kubiski, 'Alterity and the Palaiologan Hat: Dressed Otherness in the Portraits of the Byzantine Emperor John VIII by Pisanello and Filarete', in *Images of Otherness in Medieval and Early Modern Times: Exclusion, Inclusion and Assimilation*, eds. Anja Eisenbeiss and Lieselotte E. Saurma-Jeltsch (Munich, 2012), Chapter 3, pp. 73-87.

36. Glass, p. 26. See also Tanja L. Jones, 'Crusader Ideology' (2015).

37. Kafadar pp. 1-2; Harris, pp. 79-80; Crowley, pp. 53-56.

38. Babinger, pp. 31-32, 41.

39. Şahin, pp. 317-318.

40. Fleischer (2009), p. 233.

41. Babinger, Plate X, fig. a.

42. Şahin, pp. 352-353.

43. For a general commentary, see Louis Massignon, 'Textes Prémonitoires' (with thanks to Charlotte Stern for the translation).

44. Şahin, pp. 317-318.

45. Şahin, p. 322.

46. Babinger, pp. 46-47.

47. Kafadar, pp. 60-61.

48. Babinger, pp. 58-59. Amongst the mints striking coinage under Ottoman authority, following Mehmet's accession in 1444 (AH 848), were those situated at Amasya (fig. 12.1), Ayasuluk, Bursa (fig. 12.2), Edirne (fig. 12.3) and Serez (Damali 7-AM-G1; 7-AY-G1; 7-BU-G1; 7-ED-G1; and 7-SE-G1). *See also*, Nuri Pere, *Osmanlilarda Madeni Paralar: Coins of the Ottoman Empire* (Istanbul, 1968), Plate 7, Nos. 91 and 93.

49. Babinger, pp. 43-44; Necipoğlu, p. 66, n. 98. The treaty is in the Venetian State Archives, VSA, Pacta Secreta, ser. 2,

no. 230. A further Ottoman treaty with Venice in 1478, but now headed 'Pax cum Domino Mohamet Imperator Turcorum 1478', uses a similar form of address, but with the addition of Mehmet's imperial title; see Diana Gilliland Wright and Pierre A. MacKay, 'When the Serenissima and the Gran Turco Made Love: The Peace Treaty of 1478', *Studi Veneziani*, liii (2007), 262-277; Babinger, p. 59.

50. Zaho, pp. 6 and 65.

51. Armand 1: 5, 15; Hill, 33; Kress, 12; Pollard, 12; Syson and Gordon, fig. 2.19.

52. Hill, 186; Kress, 62; Pollard, 29; Syson and Gordon, 5.44; Scher (1994), 14; Scher (2019), 12.

53. Joanna Woods-Marsden, 'How Quattrocento Princes Used Art', *Renaissance Studies*, vol. 3, No. 4, December (1989), pp. 387-414, at p. 390.

54. Minou Schraven, 'Beyond the Studiolo. Ritual and Talismanic Handling of Portrait Medals in Early Modern Italy', *Numismatische Zeitschrift*, Vienna (2016), pp. 70-77, at 73-74.

55. D'Elia, p. 27.

56. Scher (1994), p. 44.

57. Vermeule, p. 263; John Pope-Hennessy, *The Portrait in the Renaissance* (1966), pp. 155-57, and p. 319, note 4.

58. The bronze relief has a weight of 184

grams, a diameter between 90.83 mm. and 91.85 mm. and a flan that is between 3.1 mm. and 7.60 mm. in depth. An x-ray fluorescence test indicates constituents of copper (90.61%), tin (5.58%), lead (2.73%) and iron (0.50%). Conducted at the University of Oxford, Research Laboratory for Archaeology and History, the help of Dr Brian Gilmour is gratefully acknowledged. For an explanation as to the general preparation and casting process for the making of medals and the use of alloys, see for example, Scher (1994), pp. 1-14; and Pollard, Appendix pp. XV-XIX and LXI-LXII.

59. Spink auction, London, 24 January 2008, 'An Important Collection of Renaissance Medals and Plaquettes', Lot 132 ('Unknown Medallist (c.1460-1470), Mohammed II, uniface lead portrait medal, 92 mm., a very fine old cast, pierced at 12 o'clock, rare'), purchased by the author. The lead relief has a weight of 246 grams, a diameter between 90.74 mm. and 91.76 mm. and a flan that is between 2.85 mm. and 8.10 mm. in depth. An x-ray fluorescence test indicates constituents of lead (89.58%), tin (9.39%), silver (0.18%) and antimony (0.15%). Conducted at the University of Oxford, Research Laboratory for Archaeology and History, the help of Dr Brian Gilmour is gratefully acknowledged. The collection from which it comes is believed to have been formed between c.1900-1928 by Count Alessandro Contini Bonacossi (1878-1955), Palazzo Capponi, Florence (information communicated by Spink). Samuel H. Kress is believed to have acquired many objects from the Bonacossi collection, including Renaissance medals, mostly now in the National Gallery of Art, Washington. Other objects from this collection are in the Uffizi Gallery, Florence, having been acquired directly from the estate in the 1990s. The Bonacossi estate is also believed to have been the source for a painting of Suleyman the Magnificent, by a follower of Gentile Bellini, which was sold by Sotheby's London on 1 May 2019, Lot 129. A detail of the Suleyman portrait is included in the present catalogue (fig. 20.1).

60. Pollard, pp. xvii and xxiii; see also, Scher (1994), pp. 13-14; and Aimee Ng, *The Pursuit of Immortality, Masterpieces from the Scher Collection of Portrait Medals* (2017), p. 23. A white chalked or inked number on the reverse of the lead relief may have served in the process of manufacture, or otherwise represents a collection inventory designation. The general absence of marks or blemishes across its soft surfaces suggests it to have seen very little handling in general over the centuries. A specimen of the relief in lead

with a 91 mm. diameter was published by George Francis Hill in *Aretuse* (1931), premier trimester, Paris, Jules Florange, unpaginated but listed under 'Quelques Medailles Italiennes, Mahomet II', where it is illustrated. Provenanced to a private collection, its present whereabouts are not known. However, its veracity as an original cast cannot be verified from the quality of the image, which is represented by a plaster. This was kindly brought to the author's attention by Richard Falkiner.

61. My thanks to Elizabeth Watkins for this and for other observations regarding the *Magnus Princeps* portrait.

62. Spinale, 'Tricaudet Medal', p. 13, confirms the kaftan's authentic style and design, and draws parallels with those pictured on later portraits of the sultan. While no kaftan with the same decoration can be found, others of similar decorative form can be found in *The Topkapi Saray Museum: Costumes, Embroideries and other Textiles*, by Hulye Tezcan and Selma Delibas, ed. and translated by J.M. Rogers (1986).

63. The piercing is a common occurrence on Renaissance medals, though one often applied with little respect to the lettering or the design, or indeed to the alignment of the portrait; see Luke Syson, pp. 231-236, 'Holes and Loops: The Display and Collection of Medals in Renaissance Italy',

Journal of Design History, vol. 15, no. 4, 'Approaches to Renaissance Consumption' (2002), 229-244. In this particular instance the importance that has been placed on the perpendicular alignment of Mehmet's portrait, as well as the intention not to obscure any of its features or the lettering, is reflected in the care taken in the positioning of the piercing, through which a suspension cord would be threaded. This can be mathematically confirmed by the simple expedient of 'squaring' the circumference of the bronze relief and then drawing intersecting diagonals from its four respective corners. Having established its geometric centre, a ninety-degree upright from those intersecting points divides the piercing at the top edge in equal measure. As would be expected of a proof or essay, the aspect is identical on the relief in lead, with the clearest indication of the importance as to how the portrait of Mehmet was to hang.

64. Taken at the same four fixed internal points, both the bronze and the lead relief measure 84 mm. from the M of the first 'Magnus' to the second S of 'Sultanus'; 85 mm. from the M of the second 'Magnus' to the T of 'Mehomet'; 85 mm. from the E of 'Et' to the T of 'Mehomet'; and 67 mm. from the stop preceding 'Sultanus' to the stop following 'Mehomet'.

65. Babinger, pp. 423-24, cites the Ottoman court historian Seyyid Lokman (1569-1597), *Personal Descriptions of the House of Osman*; no source is provided for the primary observation.

66. Spinale, pp. 12 and 13.

67. Melville-Jones, pp. 125-130 (citing Languschi); and Babinger, pp. 230, 243, 333 (referring to 'morbid corpulence and gout', but providing no primary source).

68. Ursu (editor), pp. 122-23; Freely, p. 82; Babinger, p. 424.

69. Kastritsis (2007), pp. 37-38.

70. Babinger, p. 418. For the Ottoman-Venice treaty document, see above, Note 49.

71. Babinger, p. 58.

72. Rhoads Murphey, *Exploring Ottoman Sovereignty: Tradition, Image and Practice in the Ottoman Imperial Household 1400-1800* (2008), p. 79.

73. Atil, p. 103, notes that the first such schools of painting in an imperial studio were set up in Constantinople 'perhaps as early as the 1480s'.

74. Scher (1994), p. 44.

75. For a comparison with Pisanello's medals, see for example Hill, 19, 23, 37 and 42; for a comparison with those of de' Pasti, see Hill 161, 163, 167 and 178.

76. Spinale, pp. 10-12. For the medals of Pietro da Milano, see Hill 51-56, and for the medals of Francesco Laurana, Hill, 57-65. For comparative purposes, medals by or attributed to Pietro da Milano and Francesco Laurana were examined in the collections of the British Museum, Department of Coins and Medals, in London, and the Bibliothèque Nationale, Cabinet des Médailles, in Paris. The signed medallic work of these two artists, dating to their time at the court of René d'Anjou in the early 1460s, can be characterized by designs in low relief and a quality of casting and patination that are of a variable, though frequently inferior finish

77. Pietro da Milano worked on the Rector's Palace in Ragusa, while receiving further commissions not only from the civic authorities but from the city's wealthy patrons. Kokole, figs. 1-6, illustrates some of da Milano's ornamental and figurative sculptures that graced the Rector's Palace in Ragusa. Of Pietro da Milano's work in Ragusa, only the Big and Little Fountains (c. 1441-44) and the Rector's Palace (1439-45) survive.

78. Barisa Krekic, *Dubrovnik in the 14th and 15th Centuries: A City between East and West* (University of Oklahoma Press, 1971), pp. 58-59, 136-138.

79. Hill 45, 46; Pollard 42; Syson and Gordon, fig. 5.53.

80. As well as directing the construction of Alfonso's triumphal arch, Pietro is also credited with carving sections of the arch's processional frieze, as well as the principal portraits of Alfonso, and his son and heir Ferrante I (1423-1494); see Riesenberger, 'King of the Renaissance', pp. 97-99; and figs. 21, 32-33, 40-41, 43-45.

81. Syson and Gordon, p. 233. The presence on the *Magnus Princeps* relief of the letters PM 'discreetly placed along the two folds of Mehmet's turban, in the form of a monogram, situated almost directly above his side-locks' has been seemingly noted (Baldwin's auction, 'Classic Rarities of Islamic Coinage', 25 April 2012, Lot 129 (unpaginated). However, despite careful examination, the author is unable to find any such lettering on the bronze relief or indeed evidence of it on the proof in lead.

82. Kokole, fig. 9.

83. Glass, pp. 33-35.

84. *Francesco Scalamonti: Vita Viri Clarissimi et Famosissimi Kyriaci Anconitani*, ed. Charles Mitchell and Edward W. Bodnar, *Transactions of the American Philosophical Society*, New Series, Vol. 86, No. 4 (1996), pp. i-vii+1-246, at p. 4, note 4. Mitchell, Bodnar and Foss, p. 303 (letter to Felice Feliciano, c.1457). Babinger, pp. 29-30, 44-45.

85. For Cyriacos's discussions with Alfonso on the designs and epigraphy for his triumphal arch, see Gudelj, particularly at pp. 173-174.

86. Armand 1: 6, 17; Hill 41-44; Kress 19; Pollard 21-23; Scher (2019), 10; Syson and Gordon, figs. 3.44, 3.46-3.47.

87. Raby (Scher, 1994), p. 87, provides details of the letter, of 1485, to the duke of Ferrara by the Este ambassador in Naples, which makes a reference to the request by Mehmet for such an artist, despatched as Costanzo was to Constantinople by the son of Alfonso V, Ferrante I (1458-1494). The initial request for an artist is not dated, nor do we have any firm chronological sequence for Costanzo's visit to Constantinople and the medal that he produced of Mehmet (fig. 4).

88. Spinale, p. 13.

89. Giovanni-Maria Angiolello remarked on the manner with which the young Mehmet 'seemed to be peering absently into the distance' (Ursu, pp. 122-23; Freely, p. 225); the Venetian Niccolò Sagundino, in his account of the Ottomans, reflected on the young sultan's 'melancholy nature' (Doukas, pp. 101-102); and Giacomo de Languschi recalls Mehmet as someone 'laughing seldom' and 'full of circumspection' (Melville-Jones, pp. 125-130).

90. *Bellini and the East*, p. 70; Hill, 1201; Necipoğlu, fig. 9; Raby (1987), pp. 173-174; Spinale, fig. 12. The medal is 61 mm. in diameter, cast in bronze and lead and known from a small number of specimens in each metal. Stylistic elements suggest a school or follower of the medallist Marco Guidiazini (fl. 1454-1462) and a chronology in the 1460s or later. The titulature reads MAGNUS 7 ADMIRATUS SOLDANUS MACOMET BEI [Great and Admired Sultan Mehmet Bey] and, though blundered and inaccurate, makes it clear that the portrait is intended to represent Mehmet the Conqueror, while drawing parallels between the sultan and Alexander the Great following the fall of Constantinople (Hill 30; Syson and Gordon, pp. 89-90, fig. 3.5).

91. Hill, 1202; Raby (1987), fig. 4; Spinale, figs. 5-8.

92. Diameters vary between 83 mm. and 85 mm. and there are other minor differences in detail. Hill refers to the fields of those he had seen as having been 'ruthlessly and unintelligently tooled'. The issue is thought to be seventeenth-century or later in date, but the very manner with which the surfaces of all these medals have been compromised by chasing and tooling has disguised any sense of artistic endeavour and the means of ascertaining the workshop involved in their production. Spinale (p. 12) suggests that 'Jean Tricaudet acquired a cast' of the original relief, but the absence of any direct casts, or indeed subsequent after-casts of the *Magnus Princeps* bronze relief, renders this unlikely, as certainly does the divergences between this portrait and the original. Yet while those divergences are sufficient to be able to rule out a direct casting, the portrait and the encircled titular are close enough to suggest that the source for the Tricaudet issue had to have been a sketch or draft of the original design. It is believed to have been first published by Theophile Marion Dumersan, *Histoire du Cabinet des Médailles, Antiques et Pierres Gravees* (Paris, 1838), G4, but much remains to be discovered about this issue as well as the identity of Jean Tricaudet.

93. Kafadar, pp. 93-94; Dimitri J. Kastritsis, 'The Alexander romance and the Rise of the Ottoman Empire', *Islamic Literature and Intellectual Life in Fourteenth- and Fifteenth-century Anatolia*, ed. A.C.S. Peacock and S.N. Yildiz (Würzburg, Ergon, 2016), Istanbuler Texte und Studien, pp. 243-284. For an ink portrait from the 1470s, of a heavily armed warrior of the Aqqoyunlu tribal confederation, with a feather projecting from his cap, see *Bellini and the East*, fig. 31. For further influences of Alexander

on Mehmet and the various forms that they took, see, for example, J.M. Rogers, 'Mehmed the Conqueror: Between East and West', *Bellini and the East*, p. 82; Raby (1983), 15-34, at pp. 18 and 21; and Necipoğlu, pp. 6-9.

94. Wittek, pp. 44 and 115; see also, Fleischer (2009), pp. 232-242; Inalcik, pp. 5-16; and Kafadar, pp. 3-19, 48-49, 62-90.

95. Inalcik, p. 5.

96. Armand 1: 5, 13; Hill 36; Kress, 16; Pollard 17; Syson and Gordon fig. 2.25). For a discussion of this warrior symbolism, with particular regard to the medal of Ludovico Gonzaga, see Tanja L. Jones, 'Ludovico Gonzaga and Pisanello: A Visual Campaign, Political Legitimacy and Crusader Ideology', *Arte e Iconografia* 137 (Mantua, 2014), pp. 42-57. For a broader discussion with regards to Pisanello and his chivalric designs, see Syson and Gordon, 'The Culture of Chivalry in Italy', pp. 43-86.

97. Armand I: 4, 10; Hill, 30; Kress, 9; Pollard, 9; Syson 3.5, and pp. 87-91 for a discussion of the iconography of Pisanello's medal of Leonello and its association with Alexander the Great.

98. In describing Pisanello's portrait medal of Filippo Maria Visconti, Duke of Milan, Graham Pollard refers to the manner in which the sitter's soft-top birretta reveals the hair 'shaven to the top of his ears [as being] a fashion common at the time', p. 7.

99. John Freely, p. 59.

100. 'Intelligent appreciator', Hill, p. 80. With reference to the use of the coralline elements, and its 'isolated shrub-like growth', see 'A new redemptive symbolism in Moderno's plaquettes', by Douglas Lewis and Amy Strubble, *The Medal*, 72 (2018), pp. 42-55, at pp. 46-47, fig. 7.

101. Kastritsis (2017), p. 39.

102. 'Consolidation of the Ottoman state into a formidable world empire, larger, more powerful, and more coherent than the one created by Bayezid I', Kastritsis (2007), p. 8.

103. Kritovoulos, pp. 172, 178. Michael Kritovoulos was a member of the nobility of the island of Imbros which he placed under voluntary subjugation, saving it from catastrophe at the hands of the Ottoman Turks. He was rewarded by Mehmet II, who appointed him governor of the island, in which he served until the occupation of Imbros by the Venetians.

104. Nazan Olcer, *Treasures of the Aga Khan Museum*, Preface, pp. p. xiv-xv, at p. xiv. See also Gruber, p.1, et passim.

105. Blair and Bloom, p. 24, plate 28. Three layers of superb carving,

combining vegetal motifs and calligraphic inscriptions, cover the surface of this Qur'an stand. The inscriptions include decorative arrangements of the words Allah, Ali, and Muhammad, and blessings upon the Prophet and the Twelve Imams.

106. *Treasures of the Aga Khan Museum,* 'The Word in Muslim Tradition', pp. 12-15, at p. 12.

107. Gruber, p. 1.

108. Blair, pp. 378-380, fig. 9.5. The scroll is in the Topkapi Saray Museum, # E.H. 2878. (my thanks to Sheila Blair for her communication in this regard).

109. Blair and Bloom, pp. 232–50; see also Serpil Bağcı and Zeren Tanındı, 'The Ottomans: From Mehmed II to Murad III', in Roxburgh, at pp. 262–64.

110. Anne-Marie Schimmel, 'Islamic Art', *Notable Acquisitions 1982-1983, The Metropolitan Museum of Art* (1983), at p. 10.

111. An unknown Ottoman artist: *Calligraphic Composition in the form of a Peacock*, Folio from the Bellini Album, c. 1600, Turkey, ink, opaque watercolour, and gold on paper (Metropolitan Museum of Art, New York; Louis V. Bell Fund, 1967. # 67.266.7.8r). The calligraphic master Abd al-Qadir Hisari produced calligraphic pictures of ships, respectively dated 1766 and 1766-1767 (Metropolitan Museum of Art, accession # 2003.241 and # 2014.441).

112. Spinale (p. 10) indicates the means by which the dual aspects of this feature can be read, having been positioned in such a way that on rotating the relief in a clockwise direction, *li-llah* aligns itself with 'Magnvs', at the commencement of the Latin titulature, while aligning itself once again as one arrives at 'Mehomet', and its conclusion.

113. For the extent to which the Ottomans were engaged in apocalyptic and premonitory belief, see Şahin, 'Constantinople and the End Time', particularly pp. 317-323; and more generally, Louis Massignon, 'Textes Prémonitoires'.

114. See above, Note 54, for the talismanic use of Matteo de' Pasti's medal of Sigismondo Malatesta.

115. Christiane Gruber, 'From Prayer to Protection: Amulets and Talismans in the Islamic World', pp. 33-34; Francesca Leoni (ed.), *Power and Protection: Islamic Art and the Supernatural* (2016) (exhibition catalogue, Ashmolean Museum, 27 October 2016 – 15 January 2017).

116. Porter, Saif and Savage-Smith, pp. 533, 535-537

117. Coffey, p. 80.

118. Two other talismanic swords in

the Topkapi Saray Museum collection, attributed to the ownership of Mehmet, are 125 cm and 140 cm. in length: TSM 1/90 and TSM 1/376. All three swords are made of silver, iron and bone, date to the second half of the fifteenth century and carry inscriptions in Arabic with the opening acclamation of the bismillah. The lengthiest of these inscriptions is that on TSM 1/90, which makes extensive reference to the dynastic line through which Mehmet is descended, with mention of him being the son of Sultan Osman Han's son, Orhan Han, son of Murat Han, and the son of Bayezid Han, Mehmed Han; while further expressing the hope that 'may Allah irrigate the ground of their graves' (trans.). Ahmet Ayhan, *Topkapi Sarayi Muzesi: Silan Koleksiyonu* (Istanbul, 2010), pp. 62 and 64.

119. Şen, 'Practicing Astral Magic' (Spring 2017), pp. 66-88, at p. 68. For an examination of talismanic shirts, with an emphasis on those of Murad III (r. 1574-1595), see 'Fears, Hopes, and Dreams: The Talismanic Shirts of Murad III', by Ozgen Felek, *Arabica 64* (Brill, 2017), pp. 647-672.

120. *Palace of Gold & Light*, A7 (TSM 13/408) illustrates a talismanic shirt, 135 cm. in length, which is captioned as belonging to Mehmet II, but its ownership has been attributed to Mehmet's son, Cem (information provided by Esra Müyesseroğlu, Topkapi Palace Museum).

121. Mehmet is said to have 'believed implicitly' in his court astrologer, Sheikh Akşemseddin, seeking the most auspicious time to begin the siege of Constantinople (Kritovoulos, p. 23, *f.* 55 pp.; see also Şen (2017), p. 571; and Crowley, Chapter 12, 'Omens and Potents 24-26 May 1453', pp.173-186). In his teenaged years Mehmet is reported to have displayed mystical leanings and 'consorted with Hurufi dervish missionaries', Raby (1982), p. 3. For a fuller discussion of these works covered in the Palace Library, see Cornell Fleischer (2019), *Treasures of Knowledge*, 'Learning and Sovereignty in the Fifteenth and Sixteenth Centuries', pp. 159-160.

122. Crowley, p. 205.

123. Coffey, pp. 95-96. The inscription on one late sixteenth-century undergarment suggests that it 'was meant to be worn during battle', Farhad and Bagci, p. 82, No. 4.

124. Turkish Field Ensign, silver, 15th-16th century, silver, Metropolitan Museum of Art, gift of William H. Riggs, 1913, # 14.25.466.

125. Matthew Melvin Koushki, '(De)colonizing Early Modern Occult

Philosophy' in *Magic, Ritual and Witchcraft* (Spring 2017, University of Pennsylvania Press, pp. 98-112, at pp. 108-109.

126. Guy Burak, *Treasures of Knowledge*, volume 1, 'The Section on Prayers, Invocations, Unique Qualities of the Qur'an, and Magic Squares in the Palace Library Inventory', pp. 341-366, at p. 342.

127. Monfasani (1976), p. 188, whose reference to artists working in oil is with regard to Bellini's painted portrait of Mehmet (fig. 5).

128. See Fleischer ('Ancient Wisdom'), pp. 232-233, with regard to Abd al-Rahman al-Bistami (c.1380-1455), a mystic lettrist, Arabic stylist and expert in prophetic tradition.

129. Susan Spinale describes the portrait of Mehmet on the *Magnus Princeps* bronze relief as that of the sultan in his 'youth', referring to it as having been 'executed early' in his reign, while placing a chronology on its facture in the 1460s. The suggestion that it might constitute 'an unsolicited gift' to Mehmet, by someone hoping 'to curry favour' and 'secure advantageous relations', would imply the general availability of such a portrait (Spinale, pp. 12-13). Yet all the evidence points to the *Magnus Princeps* bronze relief being a private commission by the young sultan for his own edification.

Gülru Necipoğlu has considered the possibility that the *Magnus Princeps* bronze relief might have been 'produced in the course of the gift-bearing embassies that the sultan, at the urging of his Florentine advisers, exchanged in the mid-1460s, with the rulers of Naples and Milan' (Necipoğlu, p. 21). Apart from the difficulty of squaring that chronology with Mehmet's still youthful appearance, this form of diplomatic exchange, a decade or more after the fall of Constantinople, does not seem to correspond to the absence of any imperial titulature encircling his portrait, nor with a reverse that has been left plain. Mehmet's confirmed post-conquest medals all include a reference in their titles to his position as emperor, as well as associated iconographic schemes on their respective reverses (figs. 4, 6, 7).

130. Kafadar, pp. 95-96.

131. Inalcik, pp. 20 and 22.

132. Philippides (1980), p. 59.

133. Doukas pp. 201-202; Kritovoulos, pp. 14-15, 37-38; and p. 22, 'long since elaborated'.

134. Harris, pp. 179, 182-83; and Kafadar, pp. 137 and 171.

135. Kastritsis (2007), p. 202. See also, Inalcik, p. 26; and Babinger, pp. 102 and 114.

136. Waddington, p. 9.

137. Margaret Zaho discusses at length the means with which Renaissance rulers used imagery in medallic and other forms to incorporate and manipulate the 'Roman imperial triumphal motif' in their own persona (p. 2), while satisfying the desire 'to be associated with the Imperial rulers of the past', p. 63. For aspects of Sigismondo Malatesta in particular, see pp. 67-81.

138. Douglas Lewis, 'Leon Battista Alberti (1404-1472)' in Scher (1994), pp. 41-43; Hill, 16; Syson and Gordon, fig. 3.28. For another medal of Alberti by Matteo de' Pasti, see Armand I, 17, 1; Hill 161; Kress 56 and Pollard 40.

139. Armand, 1: 6, 16; Hill 35; Kress, 15; Pollard 15; Scher (1994), 6; Scher (2019), 7; Syson and Gordon fig. 4.5, and p. 65.

140. Scher (1994), p. 51.

141. Fleischer (2009), p. 233, 'patronize various artists'; Necipoğlu, p. 2, repopulation and rebuilding of Constantinople (Istanbul).

142. Raby (1987), pp. 175-176, and 187-188; and Necipoğlu, p. 17.

143. Suheyl Unver, *Fatihin Cocukluk Defteri. Un cahier d'enfance du Sultan Mehemmed le Conquerant "Fatih"* (Istanbul, 1961); Raby (1984), p. 172; Roxburgh, p. 279. The exercise or sketch book is described by Unver as containing '60 de ces feuillets a filigrane Florentine', and is provenanced to 'des villes cotieres de l'Italie'.

144. For Mehmet as an 'awe inspiring conqueror', see Kastritsis (2017), p. 39. For parallels between Mehmet and Constantine the Great, see for example Inalcik, p. 22; and Speros Vryonis Jr, 'Byzantine Constantinople and Ottoman Istanbul: Evolution in a Millennial Imperial Iconography', 13-52, *The Ottoman City and its Parts: Urban Structure and Social Order*, eds. Irene A. Bierman, Rifa'at A. Abou-El-Haj, and Donald Preziosi (New York, 1991).

OTTOMAN REGNAL GENEALOGY

Osman (died c.1324)

Orhan (c.1324-1362)

Murad I (1362-1389)

Bayezid I (the Thunderbolt) (1389-1402)

Interregnum of Ottoman Civil War (1402-1413)

Mehmet I (1413-1421)

Murad II (1421-1451)

Mehmet II (the Conqueror) (1444-1446; 1451-1481)

Bayezid II (1481-1512)

Selim I (1512-1520)

Suleyman the Magnificent (1520-1566)

N.B. The regnal genealogy is restricted to the principal members of the male Ottoman line relevant to the present work.

ILLUSTRATIONS

1. Unidentified artist: Mehmet II, c.1450, *Magnus Princeps* bronze relief.

2. Pisanello: John VIII Palaeologus, c.1440, bronze medal.

3. Pisanello: Filippo Maria Visconti, Duke of Milan, c.1435-1440, bronze medal.

4. Costanzo da Ferrara: Mehmet II, c.1475, bronze medal.

5. Gentile Bellini: Mehmet II, c.1480, oil on canvas.

6. Gentile Bellini: Mehmet II, c.1480, bronze medal.

7. Bertoldo di Giovanni: Mehmet II, c.1480, bronze medal.

8. Unidentified artist: Mehmet II, c.1475- 80, watercolour on paper.

9. Unidentified artist: Mehmet II Smelling a Rose, c.1475-80, watercolour on paper.

10. Costanzo da Ferrara: Mehmet II, 1481, bronze medal.

11. Unidentified artist: Constantine the Great, (AD 325-370), marble bust.

12. Unidentified artist: Ottoman coinage, 1444-1445 AD (848-849 H).

13. Nakkas Osman (by or after): Mehmet II accession ceremony 1451, watercolour.

14. Pisanello: Sigismondo Malatesta, c.1445, bronze medal.

15. Matteo de' Pasti: Sigismondo Malatesta, c.1450, bronze medal.

16. Unidentified artist: Commodus, A.D. 186-190, bronze medallion.

17. Unidentified artist: Mehmet II, c.1450, *Magnus Princeps* lead relief.

18.1 (detail of 1); 18.2 (detail of 4).

19.1 (detail of 1); 19.2 (detail of 5).

20.1 Venetian, workshop or circle of Gentile Bellini: Suleyman the Magnificent, c.1520, oil on panel (detail).

20.2 Venetian, workshop or circle of Titian: Suleyman the Magnificent, c.1535, oil on canvas (detail).

21. Unidentified artist: unknown portrait, c.1460-70, bronze medal.

22. Unidentified artist: 'Tricaudet' portrait, c.1600-1700, bronze medal.

23. Pisanello: Lodovico II Gonzaga, 2nd Marquess of Mantua, c.1447-48, bronze medal.

24. Pisanello: Leonello d'Este, Marquis of Ferrara, c.1442, bronze medal.

25.1-25.5 (detail of 1, 4, 5, 7, 8).

26.1 (detail of 2); 26.2 (detail of 4).

27. Teak panel from a Persian Qur'anic prayer stand, c.1360 (detail).

28. (detail of 1).

29. (detail of 7).

30. Unknown Ottoman maker: talismanic sword of Mehmet II, steel, salmon teeth and iron, second half of the fifteenth century.

31. Unknown Ottoman maker: talismanic shirt attributed to the ownership of Mehmet II's son, Cem, 1480.

32. Unknown Ottoman maker: Turkish banner staff head, gilt-bronze, c.1675-1700.

33. Leon Battista Alberti: self-portrait, bronze relief, c.1435.

34. Pisanello: Domenico Malatesta, Lord of Cesena and Cervia, bronze medal, c.1445-1448.

35. Artist unknown, but possibly Mehmet II: drawings of heads (35.1); drawings of Mehmet's tughra (35.2), c.1445-1450 or later.

Map of the Eastern Mediterranean (prepared by Helen Stirling), p. 16.

Map of Constantinople and Pera (after Christoforo Buondelmonte), p. 26.

Map of Constantinople (prepared by Helen Stirling), p. 52.

BIBLIOGRAPHY

Armand, Alfred, *Les Médailles Italiens des quinzième et seizième siecles* (Paris, volumes I and II, 1883; volume III, 1886).

Atil, Esin, 'Ottoman Miniature Painting under Sultan Mehmed II', *Ars Orientalis*, vol. 9 (1973), 103-120.

Babinger, Franz, *Mehmed the Conqueror and His Time* (Bollinger series XCVI, Princeton, N.J. 1978).

Bellini and the East, Campbell, Caroline, and Chong, Alan (eds.) (London, 2005). The catalogue for the joint exhibition held at the Isabella Stewart Gardner Museum, Boston from 14 December 2005 - 26 March 2006 and The National Gallery, London from 12 April 2006 - 25 June 2006.

Blair, Sheila S., *Islamic Calligraphy* (Edinburgh University Press, 2007).

Blair, Sheila S. and Bloom, Jonathan M., *The Art and Architecture of Islam 1250-1800* (New Haven and London: Yale University Press, 1994).

Bodnar, Edward William (ed. and translator), *Cyriacos of Ancona: Later Travels* (2004).

Campbell, Caroline, 'Portrait of Mehmed II, 1480', in *Bellini and the East*, p. 78.

Chong, Alan, 'Gentile Bellini in Istanbul: Myths and Misunderstandings', in *Bellini and the East*, pp. 106-129.

Coffey, Heather, 'Between Amulet and Devotion; Islamic Miniature Books in the Lilly Library', *The Islamic Manuscript Tradition: Ten Centuries of Book Arts in Indiana University Collections*, ed. Christiane Gruber (Bloomington, Indiana, 2010), 78-115.

Colak, Hasan, 'Tekfur, Fasilyus and Kayser: Disdain, Negligence and Appropriation of Byzantine Imperial Titulature in the Ottoman World', *Frontiers of the Imagination: Studies in Honour of Rhoads Murphey*, ed. Marios Hadjianastasis (Leiden and Boston, 2015), 5-24.

Crowley, Roger, *Constantinople: The Last Great Siege, 1453* (2013).

Damali, Atom, *History of Ottoman Coins* (Istanbul, 2010), volume 1.

D'Elia, Anthony, *Pagan Virtue in a Christian World: Sigismondo Malatesta and the Italian Renaissance* (2016).

Doukas, *Decline and Fall of Byzantium to the Ottoman Turks,* translated by Harry J. Magoulias (Detroit, 1975).

Eimer, Christopher, 'An Early Portrait Relief of Sultan Mehmet II', *The Medal,* 74 (2019), pp. 3-20.

Eredem, H., and Fetvaci, E., *Writing History at the Ottoman Court: Editing the Past, Fashioning the Future* (Indiana, 2013).

Farhad (Massumeh) and Bagci (Serpil), *Falnama: The Book of Omens* (Washington and London, 2009).

Faroqhi (Suraya) and Neumann (Christoph K.) eds., *Ottoman Costumes from Textile to Identity* (Istanbul, 2004).

Fetvaci, Emin, 'From Print to Trace: an Ottoman Imperial Portrait Book and its Western European Models', *The Art Bulletin,* vol. 95, No. 2 (June, 2013), pp. 243-68.

Finkel, Caroline, *Osman's Dream* (2006).

Fleet, Kate, 'Early Ottoman Self-definition', *Journal of Turkish Studies* 26/1 (Harvard University, 2002), 229-238.

Fleischer, Cornell, 'Ancient Wisdom and New Sciences: Prophesies at the Ottoman Court in the Fifteenth and Early Sixteenth Centuries', *Falnama: The Book of Omens* (2009); see above, Farhad and Bagci, pp. 232-42.

----- *Treasures of Knowledge: An Inventory of the Ottoman Palace Library* (1502/3-1503/4), 2 vols. (Brill, 2019), Vol. 1, Essays, pp. 155-160.

Freely, John, *The Grand Turk: Sultan Mehmet II – Conqueror of Constantinople and Master of an Empire and Lord of Two Seas* (New York, 2009).

Glass, Robert, 'Filarete and the Invention of the Renaissance Medal', *The Medal,* 66 (2015), pp. 26-37.

Gray, Basil, 'Two Portraits of Mehmet II', *Burlington Magazine 61* (London, 1932), 4-6.

Gruber, Christiane, 'Introduction: Book Arts in Indiana University Collections', *The Islamic Manuscript Tradition: Ten Centuries of Book Arts in Indiana University Collections* (Bloomington, 2010).

Gudelj, Jasenka, 'The Triumph and the Threshold, Ciriaco d'Ancona and the Renaissance Discovery of the Ancient Arch', *Roma Moderna e Contemporanea* XXII (2014), 159-174.

Gvozdanovic, V. 'The Dalmatian Works of Pietro di Martino da Milano and the beginnings of Francesco Laurana', *Arte Lombarda,* 80-82 (1975), 113-123.

Harris, Jonathan, *The End of Byzantium* (2010).

Hill, George Francis. *A Corpus of Italian Medals of the Renaissance Before Cellini,* 2 vols. text and plates (London, 1930).

Inalcik, Halil, *The Ottoman Empire: The Classical Age 1300-1600* (London, 2000).

Jones, Tanja L., 'Crusader Ideology: Pisanello's medals in the Guanteri Chapelin Verona', *The Medal*, 66 (2015), pp. 4-12.

Kastritsis, Dimitri J., *The Sons of Bayezid: Empire Building and Representation in the Ottoman Civil War of 1402-13* (Brill: Leiden and Boston, 2007).

----- *An Early Ottoman History: The Oxford Anonymous Chronicle*, Bodleian Library, Ms. Marsh 313. Historical introduction, translation and commentary (Liverpool University Press, 2017).

Kokole, Stanko, 'Cyriacos of Ancona and the Revival of Two Forgotten Ancient Personifications in the Rector's Palace of Dubrovnik', *Renaissance Quarterly*, vol. 49, No. 2 (Summer 1996), pp. 225-267; Cambridge University Press on behalf of the Renaissance Society of America.

Kress, *Renaissance Medals from the Samuel H. Kress Collection at the National Gallery of Art*, compiled by John Graham Pollard (London, 1967).

Kritovoulos of Imbros, *History of Mehmed the Conqueror*, trans. by Charles T. Riggs (Princeton, 1954).

Leoni, Francesca (ed.), *Power and Protection: Islamic Art and the Supernatural* (2016), catalogue for the eponymous exhibition at the Ashmolean Museum, Oxford, between October 2016 - February 2017, with essays by Pierre Lory, Christiane Gruber, and Francesca Leoni; and contributions by Farouk Yahya and Venetia Porter.

Massignon, Louis, 'Textes Prémonitoires et Commentaires Mystiques Relatifs a la Prise de Constantinople Par les Turcs en 1453 (= 858 HEG)', *Opera Minora* (Dar Al-Maaref-Liban, 1953), 442-450.

Melville-Jones, John R. (trans.), *The Siege of Constantinople 1453: Seven Contemporary Accounts* (1972) (including Zorzo Dolfin's *Cronaca* and its record of the Venetian emissary Giacomo de' Languschi's eye-witness account of Mehmet).

Mitchell, Charles; Edward W. Bodnar and Clive Foss, eds. and trans., *Cyriac of Ancona: Life and Early Travels* (Cambridge, Mass. and London, 2015).

Monfasani, John, *George of Trebizond: A Biography and a Study of his Rhetoric and Logic* (Leiden, 1976).

----- (editor), *Collecteana Trapezuntiana: Texts, Documents and Bibliographies of George of Trebizond*, (Binghampton, NY, 1984).

Necipoğlu, Gülru, 'Artistic Conversations with Renaissance Italy in Mehmed II's

Constantinople', *Muqarnas: An Annual on the Visual Cultures of the Islamic World*, 29 (Boston and Leiden, 2012), 1-87.

Nicol, Donald M., *Byzantium and Venice: A Study in Diplomatic and Cultural Relations* (1988).

Palace of Gold & Light. Treasures from the Topkapi, Istanbul, published in conjunction with exhibitions at the Corcoran Gallery of Art, Washington D.C., 1 March-15 June 2000; San Diego Museum of Art, San Diego, California, 14 July-24 September 2000; and the Museum of Art, Fort Lauderdale, Florida, 15 October 2000-25 February 2001, by the Palace Arts Foundation, Chicago and London, 2002.

Pasini, Pier Giorgio, 'Matteo de' Pasti: Problems of Style and Chronology', *Studies in the History of Art*, Volume 21. Symposium Papers VIII: Italian Medals (1987), pp. 143-159 (National Gallery of Art, Washington, D.C.).

Pertusi, Agostino (editor), *Fine di Bisanzio e Fine del Mondo; Significato e Ruolo Storico delle Profezie Sulla Caduta di Constantinopoli in Oriente e in Occidente* (Rome, 1986).

Philippides, Marios, *The Fall of the Byzantine Empire: A Chronicle by George Sphrantzes 1401-1477* (trans), (Amherst, 1980).

----- *Mehmed II the Conqueror and the Fall of the Franco-Byzantine Levant to the Ottoman Turks: Some Western Views and Testimonies* (2007).

Pollard, John Graham, *Renaissance Medals: The Collection of the National Gallery of Art, Washington* (systematic catalogue), Volume One, Italy (Washington, D.C., 2007).

Porter, Venetia, Saif, Liana and Emilie Savage-Smith, 'Medieval Islamic Amulets, Talismans and Magic', *A Companion to Islamic Art and Architecture*, ed. Finbar Barry Flood and Gülru Necipoğlu (2017), pp. 522-557.

Raby, Julian, 'Mehmed II Fatih and the Fatih album', *Islamic Art* (1981), pp. 42-49 (Colloquies on Art and Archaeology in Asia, no. 10).

----- 'A Sultan of Paradox: Mehmed the Conqueror as a Patron of the Arts', *Oxford Art Journal 5*, No. 1 (1982), 3-8.

----- 'Mehmed the Conqueror's Greek Scriptorium', *Dumbarton Oaks Papers 37* (1983), 15-34.

----- 'Pride and Prejudice: Mehmed the Conqueror and the Italian Portrait Medal', *Italian Medals* (ed. J.G. Pollard). Symposium Papers VIII, (Washington, 1987), 171-192.

----- 'Costanzo da Ferrara', *The Currency of Fame* (1994), pp. 87-89; ed. Stephen Scher.

----- 'Opening Gambits', *The Sultan's Portrait: Picturing the House of Osman*, exhibition catalogue (Istanbul, 2000), 64-92.

Raby, Julian and Tanindi, Zeren, *Turkish Bookbinding in the 15ᵗʰ Century* (London, 1993).

Riesenberger, Nicole, 'King of the Renaissance: Art and Politics at the Neapolitan Court of Ferrante I, 1458-1494': 2016 doctoral thesis (https://drum.lib.umd.edu/handle/1903/18255).

Rogers, J.M. (ed.), *The Topkapi Saray Museum: The Album and Illustrated Manuscripts* (London, 1986).

----- 'Mehmed the Conqueror: Between East and West', in *Bellini and the East*, pp. 80-105.

Roxburgh, David (ed.), *Turks: A Journey of a Thousand Years, 600-1600* (London: Royal Academy of Arts, 2005).

Runciman, Steven, *The Fall of Constantinople* (Cambridge, 1990).

Şahin, Kaya, 'Constantinople and the End Time: the Ottoman Conquest as a Portent of the Last Hour', *Journal of Early Modern History 14* (Brill, Netherlands, 2010), 317-354.

Sakisian, Armenag, 'The Portraits of Mehmet II', *Burlington Magazine* 74 (1939), 172-181.

Scher, Stephen K. (ed.), *The Currency of Fame* (1994).

----- *The Scher Collection of Commemorative Medals* (The Frick Collection, published in association with D. Giles Ltd, 2019).

Şen, Ahmet Tunç, 'Reading the Stars at the Ottoman Court: Bayezid II (r.886/1481-918/1512) and His Celestial Interests', *Arabica 64* (Brill, 2017), 557-608.

----- 'Practicing Astral Magic in Sixteenth-Century Ottoman Istanbul: A Treatise on Talismans Attributed to Ibn Kemal (d. 1534)'. *Magic, Ritual and Witchcraft* (University of Pennsylvania Press, Spring 2017), pp. 66-88.

Setton, Kenneth Meyer, *The Papacy and the Levant (1204-1571)*, Vol. II, American Philosophical Society (Philadelphia, 1978), reprinted 1997.

Spinale, Susan, 'Reassessing the So-Called 'Tricaudet Medal' of Mehmed II', *The Medal*, 42 (2003), pp. 3-22.

Syson (Luke) and Gordon (Dillian), *Pisanello: Painter to the Renaissance Court* (London, 2001).

Tezcan, Hulya, *Tilsimli Gömlekler: Topkapi Sarayi Muzesi Koleksiyonundan* (Istanbul, 2011).

The Medal, Journal of the British Art Medal Society, published Spring and Autumn (London, 1982-).

Treasures of the Aga Khan Museum: Arts of the Book and Calligraphy (Sakip Sabanci Museum, Istanbul, 2010).

Treasures of Knowledge: An Inventory of the Ottoman Palace Library (1502/3-1503/4), ed., Gülru Necipoğlu, Cemal Kafadar and Cornell Fleischer, 2 vols. (Brill, 2019), Vol. 1, Essays.

Ursu, Ion (ed.), 'Journal of the Venetian adventurer Giovanni Maria Angiolello (1451-c.1525)' in *Historia Turchesca* (Bucharest, 1909), pp. 122-23.

Vermeule, III, Cornelius C., 'Graeco-Roman Asia Minor to Renaissance Italy: Medallic and Related Arts', *Studies in the History of Art*, Volume 21. Symposium Papers VIII: Italian Medals (1987), pp. 263-281 (National Gallery of Art, Washington, D.C.).

Waddington, Raymond, 'Breaking News: Representing the Islamic Other on Renaissance Medals', *The Medal,* 53 (2008), pp. 6-20.

Weiss, Roberto, *Pisanello's Medallion of the Emperor John VIII Palaeologus* (British Museum, 1966).

Wittek, Paul, *The Rise of the Ottoman Empire: Studies in the History of Turkey, Thirteenth-Fifteenth Centuries*, ed. Colin Heywood (2015).

Zaho, Margaret Ann, '*Imago Triumphalis:* The Function and Significance of Triumphal Imagery for Italian Rulers', *Renaissance and Baroque: Studies and Texts,* vol, 31, ed. Eckhard Bernstein (Peter Lang, New York, 2004).